Blue Blood on the Mat

The All-In Wrestling Story

Sir Atholl Oakeley, Bt

Foreword by

Geoff Thompson

SUMMERSDALE

Copyright © Geoff Thompson 1996

All rights reserved

No part of this may be reproduced by any means, nor transmitted, nor translated into a machine language, without the written permission of the publisher.

Summersdale Publishers
46 West Street
Chichester
West Sussex
PO19 1RP

A CIP catalogue record for this book is available from the British Library.

Printed and bound in Great Britain.

ISBN 1 873475 61 6

Mr Norman Morrell

The Author and Publishers are glad to make it clear that no reflection on Mr Norman Morrell was intended by the Author's suggestion, on page 137, that the 'Mountevans rules' were copies from the 'All-In' rules of 1930 The suggestion that the Mountevans rules, which it is now understood Mr Morrell prepared, were filched from the Author's 'All-In' rules of 1930 is entirely incorrect and steps are being taken to correct any future editions of the book. Further the 'tournament' which the Author attended, and criticised as an exhibition billed as a contest, mentioned on page 148, was held on the South Coast, and was not promoted by Mr Morrell; nor was there any intention to suggest that Mr Morrell has ever been involved in any such promotions.

To John Oakeley, and all other world champions, past and present, who, by their skill, courage and prowess, have set an example to people all over the world.

Foreword

A friend of mine, Marcus Trowler, a professional journalist and keen martial artist sent me an old copy of this wonderful book, *Blue Blood on the Mat*, last Year and inscribed it with the words 'they don't make them like this any more '. To be honest it was six months before I actually sat down to read it, but when I did I loved every page, it's one of those rare books that you just don't want to put down and when you've reached the end you want more.

I really wanted to release this book in with my own books because I felt sure that the people who read my own book *Watch My Back* would appreciate a work of this calibre. I made enquiries with the publishers and, well, here it is.

I want to dedicate this re-release to all the great men of wrestling. Hopefully, by rereleasing this great book I can re-introduce these legendary athletes to an uninitiated public that, I'm sure, will fall in love with the characters just as much as I have. Maybe it will also stir up the interest once more in the sport and art of wrestling.

It also gave me the idea of re-releasing other books about great fighters of the past who, like Mr Oakeley, are now in Val halla-warrior heaven. This then is the first in the series **Geoff Thompson's fighting greats**, and it concentrates on lesser known fighting legends of the past, their lives, their loves, their victories and their defeats. I thought it appropriate to start with Mr Oakeley because of his outstanding achievements in wrestling and also because, in his book, he introduces some of the other legends who I think you might like to read about. They say that small libraries make great men (and women), I believe this to be true, what small libraries also do is offer the reader information, knowledge and inspiration. Inspiration is the fuel that gets you to every training session and helps you to excel, perhaps helping you to push a little further each session than the last, at the end of the day if you don't have the fuel it doesn't matter whether you have a Porsche or a Lada because neither of them will go very far. So reading is an excellent form of training fuel, so do as much as you can.

After I read this book I wanted to be a wrestler, the way that they trained, the way they fought even the way that they conducted their lives outside of the arena-these guys were fighting dinosaurs and showed that, with dedication and commitment, one can achieve anything in life.

Mr Oakeley started out as a 5 stone, sickly teenager and worked himself up to a 15 stone world wrestling champion with an incredible 22" neck. He turned it around and proved that where there's a will there IS a way.

Sadly, very sadly, Mr Oakeley passed away in September 1994 at the grand old age of 85. After the 'flop' of his rival Wrestling organisation that he set up to try and combat the 'show' boys, he retired to live a quiet life in Buckinghamshire. His wife died several years before him. He has a son, John Oakeley, a yachtsman of some repute, believed to be living in Australia and a daughter that no one I spoke to knew very much about.

Mr Oakeley was so disgusted with the wrestling set up in the 50's and 60's, that he had nothing more to do with it. It is thought that he was probably one of the last Englishmen to try and wrestle or organise wrestling for REAL (that word keeps popping up in my books, doesn't it?).

The rest is better left to the words of Sir Athol Oakeley himself, I hope that, like I, you will enjoy and indeed learn from this book and that it will inspire you to do best what you best do. If you are into any form of martial training, add the art of wrestling to it- you'll be a lot better fighter and person for it.

I have left the book as it was originally written, by the expert hand of Mr Oakeley, what you read is what he thought and what he was.

Geoff Thompson. Coventry 1996

Contents

Introduction..7

1. The Mighty Men of History................................9
2. The Age of the Gorillas....................................13
3. The New Wrestling..21
4. I Turn Pro, and Mix it with the Roughest.......28
5. Karl Pojello: Intellectual of the Mat................37
6. My American Tour: Casey Berger, the Texas Champ......49
7. A Limey's Progress Through the States...........58
8. Seventeen Victories on the Trot—Then Disappointment...70
9. I Become European Heavyweight Champion...................79
10. A Brush with the Underworld............................88
11. British Wrestling Hits the Big-time..................94
12. Jack Sherry, the Greatest of Them All............102
13. The World Beater Comes to Britain................108
14. Wrestlers at Work—and at Play.......................118
15. A Muddy Interlude..126
16. Angel: the Sawn—Off Giant.............................133
17. The Post-War Scene: Competition Becomes Exhibition...141
18. The Long, the Short, and the Tallest of Them All..........149

Introduction

This story provides, I believe, an original example of domination of mind over matter. Together with the forces of hereditary ability, this enabled me, a person totally unfitted by nature to be a heavyweight fighter, to reach the top of the profession at that weight.

Providentially born into a family renowned for many famous men and women, I probably inherited my desire to excel in athletics from my grandfather, Sir Charles Oakeley, who took a great interest in the Prize Ring, and was himself an amateur heavyweight prize fighter of some repute. Sir Charles had a passion for setting up athletic records and, when an undergraduate, once drove a 'four in hand' from Hyde Park Corner to Carfax in Oxford, with only one change of horses, in six and a quarter hours. In the days when badminton was all the rage he and his brother, without stopping and without dropping it, hit a shuttlecock seventeen thousand five hundred times over the net!

On my mother's side we have the mate to Morgan the pirate as an ancestor. A master sailor and a man of great size and strength, his hereditary influence has come out in my son John Oakeley, whose sailing championship victories are remarkable both in number and variety.

My father sent me to boarding school when I was six. At eight I went to Packwood Haugh, a school at that time famous for turning out many great athletes. The headmaster, a Balliol Scholar, was also Blues. Such a school naturally attracted the sons of many famous athletes.

Until I was eleven I had taken no interest whatever in any game. My only reputation was as an undersized fighter of some ferocity. I had recently read Lorna Doone, and the magnificent account of the fight between John Ridd and Carver Doone had a deep and lasting effect on me which I retain to this day. Possibly carried away by these heroes I dislocated the thumb of the late Lord Birdwood and was nearly expelled. This unfortunate episode pro tem. ended my fighting career. However, at about that time the example of a young South African cricket prodigy, J. D. Wyatt-Smith, fired me with enthusiasm for other sports: I never looked back.

From Packwood I went to Clifton. I weighed only four-stone seven at seventeen and the school doctor put his foot on the scales at the 'medical' which I took in order to gain entry to Sandhurst. This low weight was due to the starvation we had to endure owing to the German blockade.

In my first month at the R.M.C. I put on two stone. Here I was taught to box by Jimmie Wilde. From Sandhurst I was gazetted into the Army and qualified as Physical Training Instructor. Georges Carpentier, George Hackenschmidtt and Kohlmainen of Finland were my heroes. I won a number of championships in long-distance running, also competing in the 'Marathon' for which I trained under Ahlgren of Sweden, running twenty miles a day for six months and fifty miles on Wednesdays!

My interest in fighting was as sudden as it was dramatic. Walking in plain clothes down ~ Westbourne Grove, London, one Sunday afternoon three men gave me a good beating up.

Mortified and furious I went the next morning to the Sandow Institute in St.James' Street. Eugen Sandow, himself world famous athlete of terrific strength interviewed me and when I left the Army it was under Sandow and Jim Pedley, his chief instructor, that I got my first training as a wrestler. My weight increased to twelve stone and I then began wrestling at the famous 'Ashdown Club' in Islington, so tough that it was said only three new members in each hundred ever kept their membership for more than a year.

In one open tournament I secured a headlock on Chartinet of Switzerland and he had a scissors on my ankle. Neither would give in or give way. He pulled my foot out of its socket and I rendered him unconscious for half an hour and we thought he was dead. I was adjudged the winner but spent the next two years on crutches and went back to five and a half stone.

It took four hours' exercise a day for another two years before I again reached twelve stone and recovered my strength. I also followed the body-building diet which Hackenschnlidtt had recommended in his book; this included drinking eleven pints of milk a day. I continued with this torture for a year and a half until George accidentally told me there had been a misprint in his book and it should have read five pints and not eleven!

I reduced my intake of milk and increased my training periods. Soon I was selected for the British International Amateur Wrestling team, later captained it and my career was well under way.

A.O.

1. The Mighty Men of History

Before the Prize Ring degenerated into effeminacy and bloodstained fists were wrapped in gloves, contests involving wrestling had been in existence for seven thousand years.

From the time of the Sumerians in 5000 BC the sport has been held in high esteem, both by the proletariat and royalty. Every nation in the world is known to have practised the art in one form or another.

Men wrestled long before they fought with fists. Wrestling is a sport of primordial instincts. It is also one of the most scientific of all games with its thousands of throws, counters, grips and locks, to learn all of which takes many years. Boxing has nowhere near the same number of moves.

From its earliest days, wrestling was always a major sport, even in the Middle Ages. It was a rule of prize fighting that a wrestling fall should end a round. From the Graeco-Roman era to the Lancashire Catch-as-Catch-Can period immediately preceding the Great War of 1914, wrestling flourished like no other sport.

From then, until Irslinger and I brought in the new style from America on the 15th December 1930, wrestling died in this country as well as in the United States. How this came about will be shown in later chapters.

For this is the inside story of 'All-In' wrestling. It is also the story of how it came about that I, a slightly built long-distance runner, public schoolboy, and former Army officer, first became interested in an art in which, later, I was to become the heavyweight champion of Europe and Great Britain.

You will learn the truth about this much discussed sport. How much of it is now competitive? Is it an acrobatic act under the guise of competition? Is it, like most other sports of the post-war era, just a spectacle to draw a gullible public! To be able to write authoritatively one has to be not only a champion but a life student of the subject.

The greatest of all the ancient fighters, Milo of Croton, lived in the Athenian Age. No book on wrestling would be complete without reference to this Colossus—possibly the strongest man of all time. Milo was never defeated. No modern gladiator would have lived with him for a second. His physique was Herculean, his strength fabulous.

In his time, 511 BC, wrestling was always a fight to the death. There were no holds barred. Everything went. The winner was the man who sent his opponent into eternity.

It is said that Milo became strong through resistance exercises which developed every muscle in his body. This he achieved by lifting, not metal weights, but a calf every day until it grew into a bull. Whereas a metal weight is static, a live weight, especially an animal, struggles. This exercises the muscles of the sides and develops balance. Every movement of the animal has to be resisted whereas, with a bar or dumb-bell, the muscles are worked in a straight line without variation. John Ridd in Blackmore's Lorna Doone points this out after he has seen the legs of a man working a treadmill: insufficient variation is inclined to be antagonistic to supreme strength.

Milo is also said to have carried on his head a chariot with six men seated in it; to have hurled a rock of three hundredweight for twenty feet; to have slain an ox by punching it between its eyes, and to have strangled a bull. He pulled up trees by the roots and never lost a contest or fight.

Greek and Roman alike knew the value of wrestling. In their competitive games, as well as in their training for war, they developed a system of advanced physical training superior to the methods used today in Great Britain.

It will be appreciated that wrestling requires not only balance and skill but extreme strength. In by-gone days valour in battle was useless without strength and skill. Consequently every nation in the world encouraged wrestling. Even kings, who in those days led their armies, were proficient.

Milton, in Of Education, wrote:

'Children must be practised in all the locks and grips of wrestling wherein Englishmen are wont to excel, as need may often be in fight to hug, to grapple and to close. And this, perhaps, will be enough wherein to prove and heat their single strength.'

Pepys, in his diary, tells of a wrestling match in St. James's Park in the year 1667 before the King and his nobles. It was for a purse of a thousand pounds, and Pepys says: 'Many greater sums were betted.'

It is nothing new for a baronet or a knight to be a wrestler. Sir Thomas Parkyns, who lived in Nottingham in the seventeenth century, was one. Educated at Westminster and Trinity College, Cambridge, he was an outstanding mathematician and a personal friend of Sir Isaac Newton, with whom he established an annual wrestling tournament at Bunny Park for a gold-laced hat valued at twenty-two shillings. He only engaged servants who could wrestle and who were willing to fight with him. Sir Thomas is said to have wrestled daily without a day's illness until his seventy-eighth year. 'when death gave him the back heel'. He is buried in Bunny Church where there is a figure of him in a wrestling pose. On the monuments inscribed:

'At length he falls, the long Contest is o'er
And time has thrown, whom none e'er threw before.
Yet boast not time thy Victory, for he
At last shall rise again and conquer thee.'

Perhaps the most famous description of a wrestling contest is the one in Lorna Doone, and it is based on fact. In Blackmore's story the death of the giant Carver Doone, the last of the band of robbers who lived on Exmoor during those times, is thus told by John Ridd.

'I think he knew his time was come. I think he knew from my knitted muscles, and the firm arch of my breast, and the way in which I stood; but most of all from my stern blue eyes; that he had found his master. At any rate a paleness came, an ashy paleness on his cheeks, and the vast calves of his legs bowed in, as if he were out of training.

'Seeing this, villain as he was, I offered him the first chance. I stretched forth my left hand, as I do to a weaker antagonist, and I let him have the hug of me ... But in this I was too generous having forgotten my Pistol-Wound and the cracking of one of my short lower ribs. Carver Doone caught me round the waist, with such a grip as had never yet been laid upon me.

'I heard my rib go, I grasped his arm and tore the muscle out of it (as the string comes out of an orange); then I took him by the throat, which is not allowed in wrestling; but he had snatched at mine; and now was no time of dalliance. In vain he tugged and strained, and writhed, dashed his bleeding fist into my face and flung himself on me with gnashing Jaws. Beneath the iron of my strength— for God that day was with me—I had him helpless in two minutes, and his blazing eyes lolled out.

' "I Will not harm thee any more," I cried, so far as I could for panting, the work being furious: "Carver Doone thou art beaten; own it and thank God for it; and go thy way, and repent thyself."

'It was all too late. Even if he had yielded in his ravening frenzy, for his beard was frothy as a mad dog's jowl; even if he would have owned that, for the first time in his life, he had found his master; it was all too late.

'The black bog had him by the feet; the sucking of the ground drew on him, like the thirsty lips of death. In our fury we had heeded neither wet nor dry nor thought of earth beneath us. I myself could scarcely leap, with the last spring of o'er-laboured legs, from the engulfing grave of slime. He fell back, with his swarthy breast (from which my grip had rent all clothing), like a hammock of bogoak, standing out the quagmire; and then he tossed his arms to heaven, and they were black to the elbow, and the glare of his eyes was ghastly. I could only gaze and pant; for my strength was no more than an infant's, from the fury and the horror. Scarcely could I turn away, while, joint by joint, he sank from sight.'

2. The Age of the Gorillas

The eighteenth century saw the advent of the prize ring. This flourished until the second quarter of the nineteenth century when it died, to quote Shaw, 'of its intolerable tediousness'. And tedious it undoubtedly was. Fights with bare fists went on round after round for hours. A wrestling fall ended a round. The harder a prize fighter threw his opponent, and the more times he flung him off this feet, the more exhausted became his adversary until, many rounds later, bleeding and unrecognisable, he eventually gave up. If the prize ring was killed by its boredom it lived by its ferocity.

As a means of self-defence pugilism has only since been bettered by 'La Savate' and 'Karate'. It is not generally realised that barefist fighting plus wrestling was an art which produced real champions. Men of husky physique, with strong legs and arms, barrel chests and great courage. Fists were pickled to strengthen the tissue. Men like Owen Swift, Tom Cribb, Jim Mace, Charlie Mitchell, Gentleman Jackson and others were heroes of their day. When Byron was rebuked for taking lessons from Jackson he replied that the pugilist's manners were infinitely superior to those of the Fellows of the college whom he met at High Table. The aristocracy, headed by the Prince Regent, supported the prize ring and wagered heavily on the results of matches. My grandfather, Sir Charles Oakeley, who himself stood six feet four, was not only an enthusiastic amateur and capable exponent of the noble art of prize fighting, but also attended all the big fights of his time.

Conan Doyle's Rodney Stane deals with the prize ring and has been widely read. But Boxers and their Battler by 'Thormanby', a book written long ago and passed down to me by my grandfather, gives this description which brings out the importance of wrestling in pugilism. He is referring to Owen Swift, lightweight champion of England, who, for skill, courage and ability in fighting at that weight, has probably never been equalled. Owen was champion in 1837, and had never been defeated at his weight. On the thirteenth of March, 1838, he was matched for a mill at Royston in Cambridgeshire against the Brighton lightweight 'Brighton Bill', who, under his real name of William Phelps, had killed his opponent George Daniels.

'Swift was a far more formidable customer than he looked at first sight. Every muscle in his graceful symmetrical body was fully developed. He was all wire and whipcord, with well-knit shoulders, from which his blows came like stones from a catapult.'

(It should be remembered that the rules of the ring in 1838 allowed a man to be carried to the scratch by his seconds; only much later on was this altered to rule that each man must rise from the knee of his battleholder and walk to his own side of the scratch unaided while the seconds and bottle-holder remained at their corner.)

'First blood was booked to the Brightonian who landed a right hander on Swift's mouth. The blow was not severe, but Owen's lips were chapped and it only wanted a tap to draw the claret. In the fourth round, however, the Londoner had his revenge, for, as Bill rushed in, Owen met him with right and left on the nose and ripped the skin clean off that feature. As far as ringcraft was concerned, the Brightonian was a child compared with the wily Owen, who drew his man on, artfully and cunningly, till Bill fell into the trap laid for him and dashed in only to be sent back by a blow like the kick of a horse. In the fifth round Bill was caught in this way and got a terrific smack on the jaw which knocked him clean off his feet. So the fight went on for forty minutes and, though Phelps was badly punished about the face and bleeding freely, he was still as strong as a horse and game as a pheasant. After an hour and a quarter, Phelps had both eyes almost closed and every feature of his face knocked out of shape, blood and sweat coursing down his bruised cheeks, his face a purple hue suggestive of apoplexy. Not even when Phelps was absolutely helpless, his eyes closed, his arms hanging by his sides and only just able to stand, would his backers allow him to be taken away. After the eighty-fifth round Curtis threw in the sponge. Owen had just enough strength to shake hands with his beaten foe, who tried to rise, but fell back senseless into his second's arms.

As a result of this fight 'Brighton Bill' died without recovering consciousness. Owen Swift had already killed Anthony Noon in 1834 and been tried and convicted for manslaughter, getting six months. This time he went to Paris where he fought and beat Adams. Lord Henry Seymour found the money to back Adams; the Marquis of Waterford and Lord Curgenven for Swift. Warrants were issued against both contestants. Adams went back to England but Swift dared not go back and was arrested by the French. Rather than be thrown into a French prison, Swift, after sentence, fled in disguise to England and was tried at Hertford Assizes on February 28th, 1839, and acquitted of the manslaughter of Phelps.

Owen never fought again. Thormanby writes: 'A prettier fighter was never seen in the ring during the hundred and fifty years of its history. Owen was remarkable for his marvellous quickness and precision in the use of the left, whilst he was so wonderfully active on his legs that, after delivering a blow, he was away out of danger before his adversary could touch him. At in-fighting he was equally good with both hands, the severity of his hitting was astounding and he was undoubtedly one of the best wrestlers seen in the prize ring. Add to this his admirable generalship, indomitable pluck and excellent temper, and you have the portrait of a consummate master of the art of fighting whose superior the world has never seen and perhaps will never see again.'

All through the ages, wrestling has always been the sport of Kings, and many ancient monarchs were able exponents of the art. Richard Coeur de Lion was one of the strongest men of ancient times. Henry the Eighth was an exceedingly good wrestler and competed against the King of France on the Field of the Cloth of Gold. Indian Maharajahs kept a whole stable of heavyweight wrestlers. These men have, for hundreds of years, worked many hours a day, strengthening their grips by working their hands in wet rice, then wet sand, and so on, as well as increasing their body strength, to a fantastic degree, by advanced resistance and concentration under hypnosis. They married the daughters of wrestlers and no white man, nor Japanese, has been able to defeat their champions, the product of two thousand years of inter-breeding designed to produce the super-athlete.

Stanislaus Zbyszko, when world's heavyweight champion in the Graeco-Roman and American Catch-as-Catch-Can styles, went to India for a match with the most formidable of all Indian champions, Gama. Zbyszko told me he was paid all expenses to India and back to America. The Maharajah of Patiala received him as his guest at his palace. He trained for two months, and entered the ring at twenty-three stone. For a height of five feet five inches such a weight made Zbyszko look like an egg. One could understand why no white man ever pinned his shoulders to the mat infact, at Lane's Club years later, when Zbyszko was long past his prime, Bob Gregory, myself and four other champions all tried at once to pin him. As fast as we got one shoulder down he rolled over on his face. He was in fact oval! You could not tell whether he was standing up or sitting down. His neck was two feet four around, his thighs three feet, his biceps two feet. This was the man whom Gama beat in ninety seconds. That is the calibre of the Indian wrestler. Had he won, Zbyszko would have gone home with a hundred thousand pounds. As it was he had to be content with the loser's share often thousand only.

Wrestling has always been a popular sport in Britain, long before anyone thought of soccer or cricket. It reached its peak in the early part of the twentieth century. Two people were responsible for this. George Hackenschmidt of Esthonia and C. B. Cochran of London. The former, known as the 'Russian Lion', was a magnificent figure of a man. He stood five feet nine and a halfinches. His chest measured fifty-two inches and he was as active as a tiger. Cochran, the master showman, was quick to realise the potentialities of this wonderful athlete, who had been trained as a weightlifter and who had graduated into what is known as 'Graeco-Roman' wrestling, winning tournament after tournament all over Europe. 'Graeco-Roman', for the uninitiated, is that style where only holds above the waist are allowed.

Hackenschmidt's patron, Count Ribeaupierre, had advised him to agree to the Belgian newspaper proprietor, Herr Delmer, becoming his manager and, soon afterwards, Hackenschmidt arrived in London. He was then the heavyweight champion of the world in the Graeco-Roman style. He had won the title at the Casino in Paris where Cochran had first seen but not yet met him. A heavyweight named Carkeek was appearing at the Alhambra but refused to take on the Russian until after he thought he had left the country. He then issued a general challenge. But the words were hardly out of his mouth when Hackenschmidt, accompanied by Vansittart, the strong Man of England, leapt onto the stage in full wrestling costume from the stage box. When Carkeek flatly refused to take him on there was instant and prolonged uproar. The police were called in to 'quell the disturbance and interference with the act', and Hackenschmidt was ordered to leave the stage and the theatre.

The press, however, had been quick to note what had happened and reported it the next day at some length. Cochran, who by then had been introduced to the champion, quickly took advantage of the publicity and obtained a wrestling engagement at the Tivoli at £70 a week, and this was renewed for a further four weeks at £150 a week. The sophisticated London public, inspired by the fabulous physique and agility of the athlete, turned up in thousands, and all records for receipts were broken. This engagement was followed by others in Manchester and elsewhere. Before long the name of Hackenschmidt became a household word. He was far too strong for the British heavyweights, twice beating Tom Cannon, the well-known Liverpool heavyweight. He defeated everyone else who cared to take him on. Meantime Jack Smith was training him in the new style of Catch-as-Catch-Can which had been evolved in Lancashire. In this style he defeated the Greek Peiri, but lost to Ben Olson due to an ankle injury.

The match that caused one of the greatest sensations in London was the famous fight at Olympia with Madrali, the 'Terrible Turk'. Cochran was the promoter. The Turk was huge, standing over six foot and weighing sixteen stone. He was the protege of Pieri, who had brought him in to avenge his own defeat. Everyone was sure that the Turk would end the Russian's long list of fast victories, and the house was sold out long before the day of the match. But Hackenschmidt, as the bell rang, flung himself at his opponent and, hoisting him shoulder high, sent him crashing to the mat with incredible force. Madrali lay moaning with pain, his arm broken.

No resume of events which led up to the introduction of All-In wrestling would be complete without reference to Frank Gotch, the man whom many in America still think was the greatest heavyweight of modern times in the new Catch-as-Catch-Can style.

Gotch came from Iowa and was trained from early youth by Farmer Burns, the most famous of all wrestling trainers, and inaugurator of modern American Catch. Burns had for a long time realised that 'Graeco-Roman' called for vast strength, oval-shaped men and very little skill. 'European Catch' was little better as far as heavyweights were concerned. In each of these old-fashioned styles the ruling for professionals required that the shoulders should be pinned for three seconds, while for amateurs the shoulders should touch the mat simultaneously for no more than a fraction of a second. This completely eliminated the lighter heavyweight, who had no chance whatever of pinning down the shoulders of a Colossus like Zbyszko or the giants of that period. Even under Lancashire Catch no one of my weight could hope simultaneously to pin the shoulders of a thirty-stone man. The Japanese had learnt this lesson from the Formosan heavyweights, who went up to fifty stone or about a third of a ton. Such men could not be moved by a fifteen stone man, so the wily Japanese brought in what are called 'submission holds'. These locks are so painful that, when applied to the arms, legs, and other parts of the body, they make the wrestler submit. It was these very submission holds which gave Frank Gotch the edge over Hackenschmidt in their World Title Match, in 1908, on April 3rd at Chicago.

The Chicago match has always been hotly disputed as Gotch used the toe hold, a submission lock not permitted in either European Catch or in Graeco-Roman. It was also said by some leading wrestlers of the day that the Russian Lion had recently been ill and was not the man he used to be when he first came to England. Whatever the reason, Gotch won the world's heavyweight championship in the Catch-as-Catch-Can style in a contest lasting more than two hours.

Hackenschmidt returned to Europe having undertaken to wrestle the winner of the world's championship Graeco-Roman tournament in which Padoubney, the giant Russian holder, had been disqualified in the final versus Zbyszko. Articles had been signed for Hackenschmidt to meet Zbyszko in June of 1908 but this he never did as he left the country for Aix-la-Chapelle for treatment on one of his knees.

So much for the story of Hackenschmidt. He was a sensation when he first came to England, but the advent of the giant Cossack, Padoubney, the super-hercules from Poland, Zbyszko, and technically advanced Gotch, took much of the bloom off this fifteen-stone Esthonian, who came into England like a lion and left years later like a lamb. That Hackenschmidt was a sick man when he left, as many claimed, is extremely probable according to wrestlers who knew him well. But it still remains that, in the Madrali-Hackenschmidt match, London saw an outstanding athlete.

On the departure of the Russian Lion, mighty Zbyszko came into the limelight. He was never a popular athlete with the British public, who thought he looked a cross between a gorilla and the egg of some gigantic prehistoric bird. I have seen him put on his shirt, collar, and tie without undoing them, simply by pulling them over his head, as he took them all off the night before ! With a neck over two feet in circumference, all things are possible. Cochran was the man responsible for bringing him over from Poland. Zbyszko told me he could not understand his contract and became suspicious when Cocky asked him to move from the Law Courts where he had ensconced himself to be ready for the perfidious Albion. There is no doubt that Zbyszko was a far bigger draw by and large than Hackenschmidt. The public loathed him and turned out in tens of thousands in the hope someone would beat him up. Then, when the Pole was appearing at the London Pavilion, Oswald Stoll brought in the Cossack and world champion, Ivan Padoubney, who, with Youssouf, is still considered to have been the strongest Graeco-roman heavyweight of the twentieth century. This giant quickly challenged Zbyszko and Hackenschmidt. The latter refused to accept but offered to meet the winner from Constant le Marin, Padoubney and Zbyszko. Stoll's contract with Padoubney stipulated that the Cossack should back himself with his own money, and Cochran also demanded that Zbyszko put up his own side-stake. The Pavilion management provided the house and staff, did the advertising, and took one third of the receipts. The other two thirds went to the winning wrestler, In other words the winner took all. Cochran said that never had he seen Piccadilly so crowded. Though no seat was less than a guinea, thousands were unable to obtain admittance. There has seldom if ever been a more bloodthirsty or violent fight than this. Both men were superhumanly strong and kept up a torrent of abuse in Polish and Russian. Padoubney, of gigantic height, had to stoop to get at Zbyszko's five feet five inches and could get no neck hold since the Pole's head was much smaller than his fantastic neck. But after twenty-five minutes of savagery by Padoubney, Zbyszko was in a sorry state. Blood was pouring from his nose, his mouth and his ears. His eyes were closed from forearm blows and his eyebrows were deeply cut. The audience were in a frenzy. Finally Dunning, the referee, stopped the match and disqualified Padoubney for hitting. Pandemonium broke out. Padoubney and the Russians roared execrations at Zbyszko and the Poles. No one dared go near these two infuriated creatures. Cochran saved the day by rushing down to the offices of the Sportsman, where he drew out the purse and stakes. He then came back to the Pavilion and went into the manager's office to pay Zbyszko, only to find that Padoubney and the Russians had left for the newspaper office to draw the money they thought should be theirs. C.B. did not say what happened when they found the money had been drawn! Once the money was paid over, in accordance with the referee's decision, any subsequent protest was invalid.

Meantime the audience, incorrectly convinced that the disqualification had been pre-arranged in favour of Zbyszko, were starting to tear up the seats. It was some time before the disturbance, which was near to getting completely out of hand, was finally quelled.

This sounded the death knell for wrestling matches. Although Zbyszko assured me that there was no pre-arrangement, nor could there have been with the side-stakes involved, plus the reputation of Padoubney as champion of the world, the public thought otherwise. Actually, had the match been allowed to finish, only one winner was possible as Padoubney was far superior in strength and stature to the squat Pole. But owing to this very squatness many of the throws and holds which would normally have been used by the Russian were no longer possible. He therefore used very rough methods to open up his opponent and so weaken him that he had no further stomach for resistance.

One famous wrestler who watched the match has suggested that the referee was somewhat overawed by the colossal size and strength of the contestants, and felt that the whole fight was becoming out of control with the possibility of Zbyszko, whose courage was terrific, being killed. So vicious were Padoubney's onslaughts and so furious his attacks that it may well be the referee felt he should stop it while he could.

Soon after came the Great War of 1914 and wrestling, although taught in the Army, passed into oblivion as far as this country was concerned.

3. The New Wrestling

Around 1925 Farmer Burns, the trainer of former World Champion Frank Gotch, decided that the only way in which wrestling could be re-popularised was to revise the rules of Catch-as-Catch-Can. Under the existing laws a man could only be defeated if his shoulders were simultaneously held down for a count of three'. This style had, as I have said, originated years before in Lancashire.

The Padoubney-Zbyszko fiasco had proved that, when a heavyweight developed his body until it was oval, it became a sheer impossibility simultaneously to pin down both his shoulders. In the case of Zbyszko, apart from the fact it was difficult to tell whether he was standing up or sitting down, his body was so oval that, when you pressed down his second shoulder, he just rolled over on his face.

It may well be that the arrival in America of Miyaki, the Judo wrestling champion of the world, influenced Burns in his decision to revise the rules.

Under the Japanese code a contestant could win a match by so 'locking' his opponent's arms or legs that movement or escape became impossible and submission inevitable. Although this type of lock or hold had been strictly forbidden in the old Catch-as-Catch-Can and Graeco-Roman styles, under whose rules contests were fought in the days of Hackenschmidt and the great ringmasters of that time, Burns decided that the only way to overcome the difficulty, of what he called the 'Unpinnable Pachyderm', was to include the Japanese sub-mission locks in Catch-as-Catch-Can wrestling. This he did, and the new style was named 'American Catch-as-Catch-Can', or, for short, 'American Catch'.

He did not call it 'All-In', as some people seem to think. That name was given it by Irslinger and myself, when we introduced it to England, because the new style included all the holds.

As soon as the new rules for wrestling were accepted by the American and Canadian Athletic Commissions, things began to hum.

Under the new rules wrestling soon began to recover its lost popularity in America. Crowds, thrilled by these contests, and the skill of the new world's heavyweight champion, Gus Sonnenberg, grew until 90,000 people watched his second defence of the championship.

Sonnenberg was around fifteen stone and five feet nine in height, not a big man by heavyweight wrestling standards. He was a product of the new rules, which were all in favour of the very fast and stocky fighter. The fighter who could fly at an opponent like an arrow from a bow. Who, by a series of chain holds, would wear down his opponent's resistance until, exhausted, he fell into the inevitable nap and submitted.

Gone were the days of one elephantine super-hercules whom no one could pin. Under the new rules, a stepover toe hold, crooked head scissors or Japanese leg lock made even the strongest and heaviest submit. No longer was it necessary for a man to look like an ox in order to be champion. The crowds flocked in.

Much of the popularity of American Catch was due to the extensive news-reel coverage. In London, in 1929, I saw the film of Sonnenberg's defence of his title. There was no doubt concerning its impact on critical West End audiences. They literally gasped at the speed and ferocity of the champion—a master of the spectacular flying tackle and a former all-American footballer.

I realised that the new wrestling had come to stay.

One Saturday evening, early in 1930, Bill Garnon came home, sat down in his favourite chair, and said,' I've been beaten!' 'You've been what!' I shouted.

'Beaten this afternoon at the Ashdown.'

'For heaven's sake, who beat you?'

Bill, at this period of his life, was seldom if ever beaten by anyone.

'Bloke called Sherman. Says he's an American and middleweight champion of the world.'

'How long did you go?'

'About seventeen minutes.'

'And he pinned you in seventeen minutes!'

'Well, not exactly. He used a straight scissors and neck bar. I had to quit or get my neck broken.'

'How long has the straight scissors been allowed when used with a bar!'

'Well, of course, it isn't allowed. But Sherman says that, under the new professional rules, submission holds are all now allowed as in Japanese Judo.'

'What's this Sherman like!'

'About twelve stone three or four. Very fast, but doesn't know much on his feet. Relies on a rugger tackle to bring his man down but knows a lot on the ground.'

'What about his standing throws!'

'Only double wrist lock. Doesn't seem to know or use any of the ordinary standing throws. Anyway I've asked him to lunch tomorrow. He's bringing a chap called Irslinger who came over here with him from South Africa.' 'Who and what is Irslinger?'

'Sherman says he is also American and holds the light-heavyweight championship of the world. Weighs about thirteen and a half stone I think, although I haven't met him.'

The following day, Sunday, saw the arrival at our house of Henri Irslinger and Ben Sherman. The former grim, hardfaced and outspoken. Born of a German father and English mother, Irslinger, as a sixteen-year-old baker's boy, had won an open wrestling tournament in London in 1908. In 1930 this would make him about forty years of age. I suspected he was more. Sherman was about twenty eight; swarthy and very good looking as this type of young American boy so often is. He came from Portland, Oregon, and had been an inter-collegiate champion.

After lunch Henri said to me, 'I hear you're the best prospect over here.' To which I replied, 'Well, that's a matter of opinion. I have not been beaten by anyone since 1928, if that's anything to go by.'

'Well,' said Henri, 'You're going to get beaten now. Sherman aims to try you out. Where can we go!' 'Only place is the lawn. The grass is soft.'

Irslinger was obviously not keen on this. ('We have to watch our step here. We've just come from a hot country.'

However Sherman agreed that we should try out on the lawn with Bill and Henri as judges.

As I was later to discover was the usual practice with American heavyweights, Sherman straight away started in on a furious attack, which however slowed up after the first minute when I pulled up my clenched hands into his face as he came in for a tackle. This move, which was a favourite of mine against opponents who dived for my legs, turned him a back somersault. He landed flat on his back, turned like lightning and was up on his feet again before you could say Jack Robinson.

But from then on he was more cautious and used evading tactics, foiling in quick succession standing arm rolls, leg grapevine, hank and hype until brought down with a supplice which he was unable to break. Ten minutes had then elapsed and we were both covered in mud. I called out: 'Hey Henri, time's up', but Irslinger shouted back, 'What the hell! This isn't amateur rules. Go on to a finish.'

This may have suited Sherman but it certainly did not suit me. As an amateur, my matches were limited to ten minutes. If no fall resulted the N.A.W.A. judges could give an extra five minutes and the international judges an extra ten minutes (as they did in the case of Reg Edwards). But that was all.

Here I was committed, after a Sunday lunch, to fighting a World Champion indefinitely, until one or other won. What made matters worse was that Sherman was American, and was I not pledged never to accept defeat from any U.S. citizen? To be defeated now would mean that my sarcastic gibes about the 'horizontal heavyweight horrors' of British boxing would be rammed down my throat. If Sherman beat me, as Irslinger afterwards admitted he felt certain he would, the defeat could not have been concealed for long. News like that soon spreads. And then began a fight which I have never forgotten.

Sherman was thrown time and time again, but each time and every time he hit the ground he bounced up again on his feet. The speed of his escaping tactics was terrific and more than made up for my greatly superior strength. After about twenty minutes he was still bouncing up and down and I was becoming tired. Then I slipped off a cross buttock and went down underneath. Instantly he straddled me and, with an American straight scissors, straightened me out and barred my face. The force and pain of this hold was fantastic. My face was forced into the muddy grass. My neck muscles were bursting. My body felt as if it was being stretched on the rack. Everything started to go round and round. My ear drums seemed about to burst. I was gasping for breath and still he stretched me, still he used all his force to twist my neck sideways more and more. I must have fought like a fiend. I heard Irslinger calling out the minutes as in a dream—'Twenty-two, twenty-three, twenty-four'— but at twenty-eight I was still fighting, still locked up and more furious than ever at being caught by a middleweight of only twelve stone in the same hold that had beaten Garnon. At twenty-nine I felt Sherman weakening on the head-bar although his leg scissors was as strong as ever. At thirty I could straighten my neck and at thirty-one was able to turn on my side, grab his left foot and twist it until he let go. This was the end of the fight. I got free and stood up. Sherman remained sitting on what was left of the grass and said, 'You're a tough son of a bitch and I've eaten too much lunch anyway!'

Irslinger, frowning, then called the match off. What is my opinion of Ben Sherman! Well, for his weight he was supreme. He lived for wrestling. As with many Americans his groundwork was far superior to the average British wrestler's. But his standing-work lacked variety and was inferior to that of the English champions at that weight, Jack Robinson and Richard Wills. Sherman relied on his terrific speed and wrist locks, interposed with flying tackles. He was a master at countering, and woe betide anyone who slipped off a standing hold! He made far more use of his legs than we do in England and long did I remember that straight scissors and bar.

After tea the four of us sat down to a long talk. Sherman said, 'There is no sense in your continuing as an amateur. Things have reached a state where Garnon says there are only a couple of amateurs who can give you a work out and that you travel round the country trying to goad boxers to take you on.'

Garnon grunted, 'Boxers are a waste of time. Every wrestler and rugger player knows you have only to tackle them low and hold them down.'

Irslinger went on, 'Say, listen you guys, we're not here to talk about boxing. These new rules are going to bring wrestling back on top all over the world. There ain't going to be any more small fights when wrestling gets a grip. You'll see. It'll go down and down.'

'What matters at Your time of life,' went on Sherman, Is money. This is your big chance to make use of what you have learnt. You have the ability, the looks and the physique. If you turn pro now you can show all these lousy boxers that English heavyweights are not what other countries are saying they are. Guess it's up to you to decide. If you turn it down Henri and I will be on our way. If you want to have a go, Henri will promote an open-to-all tournament for the British heavyweight championship. If, as Garnon says, you can beat all your opposition you have nothing to worry about. What do you say?'

'I can't lose anything anyway,' said Garnon. 'I'll turn pro if you will, Atholl.'

And so the great decision was made. To the utter amazement of my father, mother and relations, I, Atholl Oakeley, public schoolboy, former officer and nephew of a baronet, made English sporting history by becoming a professional wrestler!

It was decided that the new wrestling would be introduced to the British public in London at the Royal Albert Hall. Irslinger was to top the bill against Modrich, Champion of Yugoslavia. Sherman was to meet me in a match to a finish. Billy Riley was to be asked to meet Bill Garnon.

Meantime, Sherman decided that, each evening, he would take three British heavyweights and teach them the new style. Four or five were asked to turn up for trials at Mrs Hudson's gym in Victoria. From these he chose Bill Garnon, Bert Assirati (a professional) and myself for instruction. We trained nightly in the new style. Assirati was originally a professional acrobat. He was a member of the Ashdown Club but, as a professional, had not been allowed to take part in amateur competitions. In our club he and I had practised wrestling together for a number of years. As well as being a strong wrestler he was a fine weightlifter. All three of us learned a great deal from Ben Sherman.

About this time Modrich arrived in England for his match with Irslinger. He asked me to train with him. This athlete weighed seventeen stone. He was very strong and had great wrestling ability. For a long time I could do nothing with him. Time and time again I was crushed into submission. However, he was very patient and after morning and afternoon work-outs spent hours showing me how to counter holds which would be used against me when I went to America.

'You must attack more,' he would say. 'You are too slow and rely too much on strength. When you come up against someone stronger than you are, you won't know what to do.'

I can still see him, standing under the lights in the ring: his huge body relaxed as a cat but ready in a split-second to counter any hold. Modrich was not only fast but experienced. He had been taught by Pezek, whom many experts in the United States and Australia still consider to have been the most scientific wrestler in the game.

'Forget the head lock for the moment,' he went on. 'That hold is okay for some, but a guy of your height and weight cannot rely on obtaining it. Especially on the taller heavyweights who are over six feet six in height and proportionally strong. Always remember, the finest way of bringing down a man taller than yourself is the rugger tackle—down low of course below the waist. Nor can a boxer stand up to this. Once a wrestler has a boxer down he has the advantage. Boxers are useless on the ground. The "Noble Art of Self-Defence" was never boxing by itself but boxing and wrestling combined.

'By going in really low and very fast a man can be taken over. You have one or two legs trapped as he falls. All you have to do is to go forward into a "Step over toe hold" and you have him. There is no escape from that, except in exhibition wrestling where men are just demonstrating holds.'

He smiled. Whenever Modrich grinned I thought of a tiger waiting for a meal. It took me six months, being continuously beaten for two to three hours a day, before I could hold of this great wrestler. But, with instruction from Sherman and work-outs with Modrich, I rapidly increased in speed and all-round strength. Nevertheless I realised that if I was to become a great champion, I still had a very long way to go.

It is all very well being a good amateur. But for a professional fighter, boxing or wrestling must be his life. Professional champions of the world have vastly more knowledge and infinitely more experience than any amateur. In saying this I am of course referring to dedicated wrestlers and boxers. Not to those whose sole object is to make money.

In retrospect, the most important lessons, learned from Modrich, were that, while strength-super-strength-is the foundation or basis of wrestling, no one can safely rely on strength alone in order to master an opponent. It is essential to master every known throw and lock. One must execute them with speed and precision. In modern competitive wrestling (as Sherry and Pojello proved) one must be perfectly trained (as is a distance runner) for endurance. To quote Pojello: 'Only palookas have big paunches!'

4. I Turn Pro, and Mix it with the Roughest

A meeting with the press was the next move, and Irslinger informed a large gathering or reporters about his plans. They were impressed and agreed to write up the first tournament, which was to be staged at the Royal Albert Hall, London. Trevor Wignall wrote a long article, and the tag 'All-In' caught on.

Then the blow fell. Irslinger had failed to get the necessary permits for Modrich, Sherman and himself to 'work'. Henri was completely taken by surprise. When he had wrestled in London in the days of Hackenschmidt, wrestling and boxing tournaments in England were open to the world and no one was barred. Fighting was then looked upon as a sport, for which 'work permits' were not required. But now professional fighting had become 'work'. If two foreigners became finalists in a tournament, they were not Permitted to meet each other. It might put British professional heavyweights 'out of work' ! A Britisher must be a finalist. This was the official regulation which, a few months later, I fought against and won.

Irslinger and all the competitors were astounded to learn of such a regulation in this country. Moreover, while Sherman, Irslinger and Modrich were in London, no permit for them to 'work' could even be applied for, or issued. They had to leave and return. There was no time for this. Only at the last moment, before the tournament was due to start, did we hear of this regulation. Irslinger was furious. I went off to the private residence of J. R. Clynes, the Home Secretary, and argued the case for an hour. He was courteous and polite but unable to make an exception to the rule. 'It might later set a precedent!' he told me.

So the tournament had to be cancelled, leaving Trevor Wignall, and all our friends on the press, 'dangling in the air', as they put it. Sherman, Irslinger and Modrich were ordered to leave the country and that was the end of all backing by the British press for the new wrestling. They never forgave us and, except for Jack Sherry, Jack Doyle and myself, hardly any wrestlers have been publicised, or even mentioned, by the national press or members of the Boxing Writers Association.

It can well be imagined that this occurrence nearly finished, as was intended, the introduction of the new wrestling into Britain.

I rushed over to Paris and saw Irslinger, whose language was unprintable. But days later he agreed that he would return and introduce the sport to Britain with me if could get permits for the foreign fighters. He returned to London as a 'Visitor' and we set about looking for a suitable stadium.

We found two available: Olympia in London and Bellevue in Manchester. It was decided to open both, simultaneously, on December 15th, 1930.

Irslinger was to meet Modrich at Olympia by special permission. Assirati was to top the bill at Bellevue against me. This and the other match was the brain child of Irslinger, with the British fights acting as eliminating bouts for the British heavyweight championship, under the new American Catch-as-Catch-Can rules, or 'All-In' as we had named them.

So, 'All-In' was introduced on December 15th, 1930 to Great Britain by Irslinger and myself.

Both meetings were packed. Irslinger beat Modrich at Olympia in an all-action fight, the roughest ever seen in the capital since Hackenschmidt broke the arm of Pvladrali, the 'Terrible Turk' at the same hall some twenty years before. The Star gave a magnificent and eminently fair account of the fight.

At Manchester I beat Bert Assirati in twenty-three minutes before a capacity house from which hundreds had been turned away.

Irslinger was delighted, as well he might be. The next day he visited Manchester, Newcastle and other big towns anxious to cash in on the new wrestling.

In London my friend Harold Lane leased 'The London Club' in Baker Street and bought a doss house in Glasgow, then sold it and bought the Caledonian Hotel in Harpur Street, off Theobalds Road, then bought Windsor House and the Mount Royal in Oxford Street. So I was not in the least surprised, when Ted Broadribb took me and introduced me to the club, to find that Gordon's prophecies had come to pass. Harold Lane, a really grand showman who had just broken all world records by running a whist drive with eleven thousand people, was most enthusiastic about the new wrestling.

'You know, Atholl,' he said, 'this could well be the very thing we have been looking for. We have not been doing too well recently and London needs a sporting shake-up. If you would like to advise me technically I will run a show here and you can tell all these wrestlers that they are welcome to use the gymnasium here for training.

Having duly thanked Ted Broadribb for suggesting the club and for taking me in there, I rushed off to Irslinger with the news. Irslinger meantime had signed up the New St. James' Hall in Newcastle and several other halls in other cities. To get one right in the centre of London was a grand piece of luck and, soon after the Olympia opening, the first show was held at 'The London Sports Club', as the 'London Club' was now called.

Irslinger was matched with the Russian light-heavyweight champion, George Boganski, who had just arrived in this country from South Africa. Boganski was an artist in the art of wrestling, having also, like Modrich, been a pupil of Pezek. He had also been a member of Pavlova's Ballet Company and had a formidable record of victories in the light-heavyweight class. It should be borne in mind by my readers that, in wrestling, a light-heavyweight is one who weighs no more than thirteen stone nine pounds, which is virtually the same as most of the so-called heavyweights in glove fighting. At that time, Irslinger was light-heavyweight champion of the world, so the match was made at 13 st 9 lbs for the title. On the same card I fought Garnon in an eliminator for the British All-In Championship.

The match between Irslinger and Boganski was a revelation to all who saw it. A degree of skill in wrestling was shown which had rarely till then been equalled in this country. Hackenschmidt, who watched the fight, told me that Boganski was the most skilful and graceful wrestler he had seen since the days of the great Catch-as Catch-Can boom when he was champion.

My fight with Bulldog Garnon made up for its lack of professional skill by its ferocity, as the film taken at the time fully bears out. It was without doubt just about the bloodiest fight since the days of the prize ring. In the second round Garnon blacked my eye with a right hook to which I took exception and retaliated by a knuckle-screw headlock which tore his ear. As a result everything and everybody within reach, including the referee Fred Davis and myself, were smothered in blood. In All-In Wrestling it was not done to fall down on the floor of the ring screaming 'Foul' every time anyone got hurt. Nor were fights stopped because of blood. In fact at Newcastle if the fights did not get rough the fans used to chant 'We want blood, We want blood'. So Davis allowed the

Garnon-Oakeley fight to go through, which it did for one and a half hours of nothing barred, fight-to-a-finish tactics. How is it that one always gets the fiercest fights among amateurs between friends!

Garnon, heavyweight champion of Wales, from Fishguard, was without doubt one of the toughest fighters in the world. The amount of punishment that boy could assimilate, and hand out, was simply terrific. He had to be half-dead before he would give in, and had the guts to endure a fantastic beating and still come up on the winning side.

Not for nothing was Bill Garnon dubbed the 'Bulldog', and I was lucky to obtain the decision over him. There were times when it seemed I would have to kill him before he would give way. As it was I caught him in a Japanese leg lock (later to be used by the immortal world heavyweight champion, Jack Sherry) from which there is no escape. Even so Bill would not give a submission, but Fred Davis held he could not escape and gave the fall to me and the match.

Afterwards for good measure I issued a challenge of £500 to all British boxers or anyone else who could stay thirty minutes with me, all in, nothing barred, with or without gloves, without getting knocked out or made to quit. This was mainly because one of the boxing writers, whose job (it then seemed to me) was to prepublicise professional boxing, had described Modrich and Irslinger as 'tigers without teeth or claws'. Well, they found out that one British wrestler at least had plenty of teeth and claws and was quite prepared to use them on any glove man who wanted to try. While three, later, took up this challenge by Jack Sherry, and got beaten very quickly, only one took up mine, and that an American middle-weight who also got beaten with and without gloves.

Soon after this, having beaten the opposition in the heavyweight and light-heavyweight divisions, I was matched by Irslinger with George Boganski at Lane's Club. This match taught me the difference between a really good amateur and a first-class professional. Boganski, a notoriously clever and brutal fighter, was determined to teach me a lesson I would not in a hurry forget. 'You b— he said. 'You just like hurting people. You no care what you do so long as you vin. I know all about you. I see you mit poor Garnon. You like blood. Vell now you get blood. Plenty of blood. Your blood. You remember the great George Boganski long time. You see, you be sorry Irslinger make this match. I show you up to your friends. They see you only palooka when you meet Boganski. You withdraw now while plenty of time.

None of this talk really perturbed me. I thought Boganski was the 'Russian Wash' because he was afraid I would beat him and wanted Irslinger to give him a new opponent.

Lane's London Club was again packed for the fight. Everyone was a little tired of my 'knocking' of the British heavyweight boxers who ruined the prestige of Britain in the USA by going over there and getting knocked out. So they came along for a Roman Holiday to see me get the good thrashing which Hackenschmidt had assured a number I was certain to get from the Russian.

Nor were they to be disappointed. Fred Davis was again the referee and cautioned both of us against breach of the rules, particularly the Flying Mare, used palm uppermost, and other bone breaking holds. Boganski said to him, 'What you think I am? A - amateur?'

The bell went and two seconds later I was flat on my back from a right cross, bare fist. Davis stopped the fight and said to Boganski, 'Now listen to me, George. This isn't a prize fight and in this country we do not allow the use of the bare fist. If you don't behave yourself I'll have you out and give Oakeley the verdict.' Not understanding Russian, Boganski's rejoinder to this made no impression on us. The fight continued.

In the course of it I got all Boganski said I would. In one round he held me in a short-arm scissors like a vice and then hit me time and again in the face and stomach till my head reeled and I really wished myself dead. All the time he was saying, 'Quit, you bloody Britisher! Quit like all the others.' Time and time again Davis asked me if I had had enough. Under the rules of the British Wrestling Association, an independent body set up by Irslinger, no single judge could give a points decision. As in the Olympiad, a majority vote had to be obtained, and this meant three judges. So it was that in a fight lasting one hour ten minutes I tasted defeat for the first time.

Meantime other halls were opening up, not all of them very successfully. At New St. James' Hall in Newcastle, Irslinger sent George Boganski up to top the bill. George had been telling Irslinger for some time what a great draw he was and that the crowds in Lane's Sports Club had all come to see him. So Irslinger said, 'Okay, George, you're such a good draw you can fight in Newcastle and I'll give you a percentage. You take ten per cent and pay your own fare.' George thought this fine but not so fine when he arrived back in London with a net profit of one shilling and tenpence. 'What you moaning about!' asked Henri. 'I always told you that was what you were worth.'

On one occasion Jack Ansell, Boganski's trainer and manager in England, came into Lane's Club and spoke to me for an hour. He suddenly said, 'I'll have to go now. I left George running round the park but I expect he has gone home and is waiting for me.' When Jack got back he found Boganski still running round Clapham Common. He had been doing this for three hours. 'I was waiting for you to tell me to stop,' said George.

Norman Ansell, brother of Jack, was trained by Boganski and Irslinger put him on in Newcastle. He was rather tame so I suggested he buy himself a yellow dressing gown, yellow pants and put a skull and crossbones on it. Norman reluctantly agreed to this and also to my suggestion that Norman the Butcher should be printed in large letters on the back of his gown.

The Newcastle press wrote: 'Norman Ansell, now called "Norman the Butcher" (Heaven knows why), wrestled well and cleanly to beat'

However, under the tuition of Boganski, Norman the Butcher soon learned to live up to his name, and, with Jack Pye, whom I nicknamed 'The Doncaster Panther', soon became world famous. No one who saw these two in action will ever forget them. Tremendous crowd pullers, fantastic fighters, they make the present-day herd of acrobats look like a mothers' meeting.

While all this had been going on Irslinger had opened up the New Victoria Halls at Nottingham in a very big way and was drawing large crowds. One of our best amateurs had turned professional on my recommendation and I had nicknamed him 'King' Curtis, the latter being his real name. King was a heavy, powerful wrestler and a great fighter. Lazzerini, the Nottingham promoter, was to my mind giving too much to Irslinger, and I thought he needed gingering up. So I got Curtis to write to the Nottingham paper and say that it was about time they had some wrestlers on. This annoyed Henri who had been having things all his own way, and quietly making a lot of money. When he read the notice in the press, which, as usual, being inspired by me, was fairly rude and outspoken, Irslinger immediately told Lazzerini to send King up and he would wipe the floor with him in the best Irslinger manner. King, however was a full-blown heavyweight of sixteen stone whereas Irslinger was only by comparison quite a little chap of 13 st 9 lbs. There was a right royal set-to in front of a packed house and the great Henri only managed to win with very considerable difficulty against the formidable Curtis. In fact, had King then known as much about wrestling as he knew five years later I think Irslinger would have been unable to give away so much weight to him.

Meantime Boganski had worked himself up to be Newcastle's star attraction, challenging the world and beating all the Northern opposition who took him on. At each victory he made more and more money on his percentage and got more and more conceited. About this time I had decided on Irslinger's advice to go to America and take all comers, but before this was possible it was absolutely necessary to beat Boganski. With this in mind I trained even more assiduously, six and seven hours a day, and finally issued a challenge via the Newcastle press. Boganski, sensing the crowd that a return match between the British champion and himself would draw, and as usual feeling he was a certain winner, promptly accepted. Irslinger agreed to the match and undertook to hold the side-stake of a hundred guineas.

Before a capacity crowd of over five thousand chanting, 'Blood, we want blood' Boganski gave them all they asked for but, in the fifth of the six ten-minute rounds, got careless and was caught in a headlock with which I wellnigh broke his neck, so frightened was I that he would pull out. Like all other 'Boganski Fights' with people he disliked, this was another bloody affair. I had a cut on my head and a bleeding nose in the first round, after a very tame four minutes, when you could have heard a pin drop.

At this early stage some merriment was caused by a local wag who roared out, 'Hey, Ref, stop it; it's murder'! This brought the house down and so incensed Boganski that he started in with fists and everything else. So the locals got what they asked for.

Meantime Irslinger, having disposed of King Curtis, decided he would offer me a fight for the world light-heavyweight crown of which he was the holder. In those days, although I was the British heavyweight champion, I also held the light-heavyweight title. My weight, which was later to rise to fifteen stone in the USA, was then only thirteen stone nine pounds. I was thus qualified to fight Irslinger for the world title. The match, after much argument as to the referee, was scheduled to take place at Nottingham in 1931, before I left for

America. It was of considerable importance, so the former world heavyweight champion, Stanislaus Zbyszko of Poland, was asked to come over from America to referee.

On arrival in England he first went to see Irslinger and then came to see me. No words can describe this enormous man. His thighs were three feet round, his calves twenty-one inches, his neck two feet and three inches, his chest seventy-five inches. His weight was 23 st 5 lbs. He sat on our sofa and broke it. He rode in our car and the springs had to be reset.

The next day, Stanislaus said he would like a work-out so I took him to Lanes Club. The courageous 'Bulldog' Bill Garnon offered to take him on and was at once hauled into the crushing tree-like arms of Zbyszko and laid gently down, as a mother lays down her newborn baby. Then, with twenty-three stone on top of him, Bill decided to call it a day. After this the wrestlers held a consultation and decided that six at once might do the trick. So we collected, Bob Gregory, Harry Brookes of Huddersfield, myself and two others. With Garnon all of us attacked Zbyszko at the same time but he flung us off individually as a bear throws off hunting dogs. Finally he said he would go on his knees for us but even so we could not turn him. So he said he would lie on one shoulder and we could pin the other. All six of us put all our strength and weight on his shoulder and bit by bit down it went. Just before it touched, over rolled this eggshaped man on to his stomach, and, with six heavyweights hanging on him, stood up, shook his shoulders and threw everyone off.

To continue with my story. The great day drew near and Nottingham was in a ferment. Wrestling fans are not likely to forget this fight. There were people sitting in every conceivable part of the New Victoria Halls, above and below. Crowds were turned away. We entered the ring. Zbyszko followed. I can still hear the gasps of utter amazement which greeted his arrival. The steps of the ring creaked under his colossal weight. Irslinger in long black tights had a white towel dressing gown on and a hot towel round his head. Zbyszko brought us to the centre of the ring and told a second to dry Henri off. He then tested him for grease and had him wiped down all over. He then tested his hair, and then his body for resin. (Some wrestlers have been known to use chloroform on their hair.) He then did the same for me. He asked me why I had knee pads. I told him. He said, 'I thought those were for cricket.' The bell rang for Round One.

Irslinger flew out of his corner like a guided missile, raining blows on me with his forearms. I was driven by the ferocity of his attack into my corner and could not get out. I thought, 'Fight, I must fight. This will be over in another minute if I don't.' The crowd were in a frenzy, standing on the chairs and yelling for me to fight. In two minutes blood was pouring from my nose and ears. I slumped to the ground and Irslinger attempted a crooked head scissors, but I slipped out of the ring into the audience. The din was deafening. It shook the building from top to bottom. All I could see through blood-blinded eyes was a mad mob seething with hatred for Irslinger and his tactics and willing, with all their might, that their flaxen-haired champion would do something. How I weathered that first round I shall never know. The ferocity of Irslinger made Boganski's efforts seem like child's play. Like all American champions he put all he had into those first ten minutes. Afterwards he said to Sherman he never could understand how I survived the first ten-minute round. But I did. Irslinger however put colossal efforts in the second and, in the third, pinned me flat to the blood-spattered canvas. Zbyszko held up his hand. Henri, scowling at the ear-splitting boos of the partisan crowd, walked to his corner and was swathed in towels.

Henri, sure of victory (how many fighters make this mistake?), came out for the fourth ten-minute round and tried something I had never seen before: an ankle lock plus grapevine. I went down like a felled ox, twisted, and crawled under the ropes. Stanislaus made us stand up in the ring. Irslinger tried it again but I foiled it, and thereafter regained my confidence. What had I to lose! Irslinger was world champion with years of experience all over the world. I was an ex-amateur. No one expected me to win. So I trusted to my hard training and attacked. Irslinger, shaken at this change, backpedaled and seemed to tire. By Round Six he was a very tired, and (I thought) a rather old man. I pinned him in the fifty-fourth minute of the match. The crowd went completely mad. Even Zbyzsko was smiling. To me this was the turning point of my whole career. I had held the reigning world champion to a draw with an American referee whose impartiality was a feature of the fight. I knew then that my ambition to Prove to the world that an English heavyweight could lick the Americans in their own country would come true.

5. Karl Pojello: Intellectual of the Mat

During the events described in the last chapter, arrangements had been completed for my visit to the United States. Mr and Mrs Alfred Pike of Pelham Manor, New York City, had invited me to their house during my stay in America. I was warned not to go without an American manager—a mistake so often made by British heavyweight boxers—and I signed a contract with Harry Garsh, the manager of world champion boxer, Harry Flowen.

Harry Garsh was an astute man of the, world—the American world. He knew the ropes. It was agreed that I would challenge all comers more diligently than did Harry. Not only had he arranged for my training quarters but he had also invited the American press to meet me on my arrival. Secretly he may well have been rather amused at this chance to act for a wrestler—the first English wrestler to visit the States and compete in the heavyweight division.

I left England in the Honteric, the yacht formerly owned by the German Kaiser, Wilhelm II, and now converted to a liner. As the shores around the Solent disappeared, on that spring day in 1931, it never occurred to me that I might be biting off more than I could chew. Such is the optimism of youth! On looking back it seems a colossal piece of cheek even to have attempted what all other British heavyweights had failed to do.

It is one thing to take on Americans, brought over to Britain on a work permit, but quite another to go into their territory and challenge champions, on their own ground and before their own people.

Nothing is made easy for the foreigner. With some twenty thousand or more heavyweights in wrestling and in boxing, even the so called 'second raters' on their own ground can and have for years made small fry of British heavyweights, notable exceptions being Tommy Farr (who went to the top and greatly enhanced the reputation of the British in America) and the old-timer Bob Fitzsimmons.

After an uneventful voyage we made a far from uneventful arrival. The American press, plus Harry Garsh, were there in force. Questions were fired at me from all sides. 'How long do you intend to stay, Captain? "Harry, please tell them I am not a captain.' 'Okay, Cap, so you're not. Maybe I should have made you an admiral.'

'I never told you I was a captain.'

'You did, boy. You said you was captain of some team.'

'Yes but that's not the same as being a captain in the Army'.

'Who cares anyway,' said someone else, 'Tell us, Cap, how long do you intend to stay over here?'

'Until I'm beaten.'

'Say, if that's so you can book a reservation right now.' Other questions followed one after another in quick succession. 'Who sent you over, the King!' 'What happened to jolly old phainting Phil!'

'Harry says you've come here to show up your boxers.'

'When are you guys going to pay us back the money we lent you for the Kaiser's war?'

'Say, Cap, where's your high hat!' (a reference to Ramsay MacDonald and Co. who had arrived in top hats and had them knocked in as they went down the gangplank).

'How much you weigh' You don't look like a heavyweight to me,' and so on and so on.

Harry Garsh was right on the ball with these fellows. Nevertheless I must admit to being glad when we eventually arrived at Pelham Manor. New York was then, as now, a fantastic sight. The view of all the huge skyscrapers as we entered the Hudson was like something out of fairyland. These were the days of Dutch Schultz and Al Capone. The days of Prohibition. Gang fights to the death were commonplace. Each gang had its own territory. Capone in Chicago, Schultz in New York, and woe betide anyone who muscled in on the other's territory.

I arrived at Pike's and soon settled in. The next day Harry called me, and came round in his car. He took me down-town to meet Jack Curley, the 'Baron of Wrestling'. Jack was equally well known as a leading boxing promoter second only to Tex Rickard. 'Hiya, Jack?' said Garsh. A huge man sitting behind a very large desk rose to meet us. Besides his size the most noticeable thing about him was his beautifully cut suit.

'Yes, it's Savile Row,' he said.

Around the office were wrestlers. But boy! oh boy ! what wrestlers ! Never in my wildest dreams had I ever imagined the colossal physique of these men. The fabulous German, Hans Steinke, had to be seen to be believed. He literally towered over me as we shook hands. That is if you can call a grip like a gorilla's 'shaking hands'. His great height and monstrous chest made me feel like a pygmy. Beside him Garsh looked like a small boy. I could believe the story told me later of how Steinke, not being given the wrestling purse that he had expected, gripped one of the managers by the seat of his trousers and, with one hand, held him outside this eighth storey window all the time threatening to open his giant fist unless he was paid the amount promised him.

Need it be said that this was agreed without further argument?

'Welcome to America,' said Curley, extending a hand nearly as large as that of Steinke's. I sat down in the chair he offered. Garsh sat beside me.

'Now listen to me, Cap,' Curley was smiling, 'You don't look much like a heavyweight. Maybe in England, yes. Over here no one under two hundred can compete in the big division. How much do you weigh?'

'One hundred and ninety but I can probably make two hundred by the time you match me.'

'Say, I guess that's the minimum for heavyweight wrestlers over here.'

I quickly replied: 'If two hundred pounds is the lower limit how about Jack Dempsey!'

'Waal, it's like this. Jack is a fighter and boxers are lighter than wrestlers. I guess Jack was no more than one eighty-five although he looks more and has the height. How tall are you, Cap!' 'Same as Hackenschmidt, five feet nine and a half.'

'Maybe so but when Hack met Frank Gotch he weighed two fifteen.'

'Sandow was one eighty when he came to USA.'

'Sandow was not a wrestler. You are. Now listen, Cap,' Curley went on, 'I know all about you. How you beat Boganski, and are joint world light-heavyweight holder with Henri. But these men here are bigger and much stronger than both you and Irslinger put together.'

'And much slower,' I interrupted.

'Don't count on that, Cap,' replied Curley. 'These guys can make rings round the kind of heavyweight fighter you have over in England. Now the Lithuanian champion, Karl Pojello, is about your height, but he is heavier. I aim to put you under him so that you can learn our new style. It is different to your European Catch. Over here we have Judo-holds, locks and submissions, all in as you know.'

I stood my ground.

Eugene Sandow, under whose instruction the author had his first training session as a wrestler.

'I am prepared to meet anyone. My motto is and always will be, "No one barred".' Garsh chuckled. I went on passionately: 'People in England are sick and tired of so called "fighters" who go to America and disgrace us with their performance. It is shocking bad publicity for a brave people. It makes a laughing-stock of us everywhere. I am here to prove that there is still plenty of life left in the old country.'

'Okay, okay, Cap, we know all that. But you should figure out what you're taking on.'

To which I replied: 'Jack, for seven years I spent four hours a day building myself up for this. No referee will have to stop the fight in case I get hurt.'

'I'll go along some of the way with that, Cap,' said Curley, 'but not all the way. 'What about Jackie (Kid) Berg for one? There's a fighter if you like.'

'Kid Berg,' I replied. 'Driscoll, Wilde, Relwyskow and Fitzsimmons. All are supreme fighters, but none of them were or are heavyweights.'

'Well, you may be right, boy, but first let me tell you a story. Some time ago the then British Heavyweight Champion Wrestler, Tom Cannon, and two other wrestlers, all big men, with much the same crazy ideas as you have, went along to a Garden Party given by the Maharajah of Patiala. It had been advertised that the Maharajah would give ten thousand pounds and a load of jewels to anyone in the world who could stand up for three minutes to any of his great Indian heavyweights. Tom and his buddies figured on collecting some easy dough. They took off their Navy uniforms and put on ordinary clothes. Then they went along to the Maharajah's party ready to collect. Just like you, they guessed these guys were big muscle-bound bums who were ripe for a push-over. Then in walked the Hindoos. All stood over six feet five and weighed 280 or more pounds. Their chests were like barrels. Their arms and legs like trunks of trees. Tom and his friends could not believe their eyes and right away decided the Maharajah's dough and his jewels were not for them. They made a fast get-away. Maybe, Cap, when you see what we have in store for you, you too will act like Tom did and return to jolly old London while you still have the chance and before you get hurt.'

This speech needled me and brought a roar of laughter from some wrestlers who had been following the conversation.

I angrily retorted, 'I never quit. Anyway it is all fixed, isn't it! Fix it for me to win or not I shall win anyway.' This staggering piece of insolence and bombast (I well remember the astonishment with which it was received) brought just one reply which those newspaper cynics (who believe everything in professional wrestling here and in USA is fixed) might well remember. It was: 'Come now, Cap, even you cannot believe that we would fix for a Britisher to win over an American here in our own country. You sure must be joking!' He went on: 'We admire your guts in coming over here at your own expense to challenge our best, but look around. You are only a small guy among a heap of big guys. What can you do against this kind of fighter? Heavyweights come here from all over the world for big money. Heavyweights with class can make plenty of dough, more so than any place else, but you gotta have strength and size. Skill alone won't get you anywhere over here. All the same, our old friend Harry here is looking after you. We know your record. If you were a palooka he would not go all out for you the way he has. Sure we'll give you a break but I warn you it won't be no pushover. We'll give you all the publicity you want. If you put up a fight against one of our champions we'll give you another fight later on against some light-heavyweight. But no Britisher is going to come over here trying to make a monkey out of us. So I'm warning you, if you want to get out now, you're free to go. We'll say you was ill or something. You ate something bad. We'll fix it real good, Cap, and pay your trip home. Take my advice. What you say, Harry?' Garsh said, 'I guess it's up to Cap'.

I said, I'm staying, Jack.'

So ended the first interview with one who, with Tex Rickard, was one of America's greatest fight promoters, himself both a wrestler and a boxer.

'Who will take the mat with Hinderscmidt?' Taken from the Daily Sketch, November 1907. (1) Vervet (left) and Bachier, of France; (2) Zbyszco (on top) and Vervet; (3) Zbyszco (left) and Fossleitner; (4) Kahouta (on top) and Peter Gotz.

Curley was right in what he said. But I had come to fight and fight I would, so Harry and I went off for a coffee. Here Harry, after telling: me not to drink the iced water the Americans always put on the tables, said: 'Say, Cap, have you always been so dog-gone stubborn! If you're thinking of me don't worry yourself. I just don't want to see you get hurt.'

'Harry,' I replied. 'In my World Championship fight at Nottingham, England, when I tied with Irslinger, Zbyszko the referee will tell you that after sixty minutes there was not one inch of the canvas which was not red with blood. My blood. My father brought me up never to quit. I am going through with my challenge to all heavyweight boxers or wrestlers in the States.'

'Okay, Cap. If that's the way your feel let's go to Bothner's and see Pojello.'

Karl Pojello was born in Lithuania, which is now Soviet territory. He was my height and externally looked like a university professor. He wore gloves and dressed in a long blue-grey overcoat and homburg hat. He spoke very softly, almost over-politely, with a Russian-American accent. He was fluent in no fewer than six languages. He was also a fully qualified chemist.

If you had to take a sock at anyone in a bar, Karl would probably have been the person you would have chosen. He looked as if he had never taken a day's exercise in his life. Something between a politician and a professor, quiet and good-looking.

Never was there such an illusion, as many had found out to their cost. Beneath this exterior he was a concentrated, dynamic ball of muscle, and as supple as a tiger. Karl had actually been in a St. Petersberg Hotel the very morning that the Bolshevik Revolution had broken out. After narrowly escaping the Red soldiers he walked one thousand five hundred miles, until he reached Paris. Shortly afterwards he left for America where he became an American citizen.

Karl was one of the most courteous and kindest of men. But if attacked he was the deadliest. He could break your neck, arm, or leg so fast that you would not even see the move. But he never attacked and he never kicked. He just waited for an opponent to touch him. The second he felt a hand on him, over his head he took you and slammed you to the ground. Not only was he a man of immense latent strength but all his throws were perfectly executed with wonderful timing and terrific speed. Unless you were a very experienced wrestler indeed you had no chance at all. If you aimed a blow at him he would instantly catch your fist and break your arm like a matchstick. This was the description given me by a then well-known Chicago gangster. He had tried to get Karl to protect him after seeing such a move actually executed on a boxer. So great was Pojello's reputation at this time that no heavyweight boxer in the world would take him on. He had even toured Japan taking on champions in Judo and Karate and defeating them. During the Second World War, at the request of Eisenhower, and to test the strength of Japanese experts, Pojello at 64, took on in front of high-ranking officers of the General Staff, the twenty-eight-year-old Karate/Judo champion proving that these forms of self-defense were both inferior to wrestling and their efficiency greatly exaggerated.

Much later, when Karl was in London, we were in a pub at the top of St Martin's Lane. A man said, 'I hate the guts of these bloody Russians. They are all the same. A bunch of murderers.' Karl turned round and said very quietly, 'You no say bad things about other peoples. All nations have some good, some bad. Peoples are not bad because they belong to one country.'

The man (a very rough-looking type, tall and heavy) looked at Karl. He said, 'You get the hellouta here. We don't want any bloody communists here.'

Karl replied, again very quietly, 'No, sir, I no get out. I like very much this place.' To which he got, 'You get out or I'll do you.' Karl smiled. Then without warning the man struck at him with a right cross. Believe you me, friends, it was some punch! Like a flash Pojello turned into it. His assailant was hurled, literally hurled, right through the door and out into the street, where he lay with his right arm broken. Karl said, 'I very sorry I hurt you but you must learn not hit peoples you not know and who do you no harm.' I got a taxi and we took him to hospital, where Karl paid his fees.

Some years afterwards I met the same man. He said, 'Bloody marvellous, mate. I remember trying to hit him and knew nothing more till I found myself in the street with a busted arm.'

This was the type of man Curley had chosen to train me. Perhaps a better phrase would be to 'tame' me. I met Pojello at George Bothner's gym. Bothner, ex-lightweight champion wrestler of the world, was then around ninety and wrestling daily to keep fit. The gym was full of fighting celebrities, and amongst those I met was Jack Johnson, the greatest of all heavyweight boxers, now aged seventy. No boxer there could land a glove on him. He offered five dollars to anyone who could punch him on the nose. No one succeeded. That was the class of fighter in those days. Compared with Johnson (and I have seen them all) modern boxers are amateurs.

My work-outs with Pojello showed me how very little British fighters knew compared with the Americans. He wrestled in an entirely different style to that in which I had been trained. Whereas competitive British wrestlers relied upon strength to wear down their opponents, so obtaining holds by force, Pojello taught me that you only use force to counter, or after you have used strategy to lure your man into a vulnerable position. Chain holds (i.e. a succession of holds one after the other in quick succession) were unknown in England except in acrobatic exhibitions.

In the amateur game British champion wrestlers were taught to go all out for ten minutes. They had to use every endeavour to obtain a flat fall. This could be likened to an athlete running a hundred yards. As Pojello said: 'One supreme effort and you are exhausted.' He taught me that the correct way to fight a champion is to wrestle within your capabilities just as an athlete runs a mile. The latter does not go off like a bull at a gate. During earlier laps he does no more than keep up with his leaders. In this way he keeps in reserve a great store of energy for the final dynamic run in. By forcing his opponents along at a fast pace, without attempting to lead them, he wears them down. When the bell goes he makes a concentrated effort and runs in, past all the leaders who, by that time, are exhausted.

This was the principle of the new wrestling. You have to conserve your powers for the final effort. Having worn a dangerous opponent down by punishing holds, you find that his muscles become tired and his resistance exhausted. Then all you have to do is to pick him up and slam him. The final shock of the fall takes all the fight out of him.

This was the Pojello doctrine for use against highly experienced wrestlers. But in the case of an experienced boxer one must tackle him low as in rugger. This nullifies his punching power and brings him to the ground. You then scissors him round the neck with your legs at the same time using a double wrist lock to stretch his arm back and out. This is a lethal hold called the 'crooked head scissors'. With this lock it is very easy to break his arm, dislocate it, or break his neck in a matter of seconds if you wish. No one caught in this way by me ever argued, I can assure you!

When I first began my training, Pojello, to illustrate the point, invited me to attack. He made no initial resistance until the moment when I had one of his shoulders on the mat. Then with supreme effort he caught me in his scissors hold, afterwards literally bouncing to his feet like an India-rubber ball! Invariably he would allow me to pick him up and slam him, or bring him down with a 'double wrist lock' or 'cross buttock'. Only when he struck the ground did he bounce up with a single movement on to his feet. Ten minutes spent in throwing fifteen stone all over the mat was exhausting and more than enough for me. Aching all over, out of breath and hardly able to stand up, I could offer no resistance when Pojello stepped in and pinned me.

This new style brought in an entirely different type of wrestler. It greatly speeded up the action. Two elephants matched against each other both use strength simultaneously and nothing much happens. This was what occurred in the days of Hackenschmidt in the Zbyszko-Padoubny match at the Alhambra in 1911 These huge men stood for an hour with neither giving way at all. Both used strength and weight. Even the mauling and punishment which each handed out to the other got them nowhere. Zbyszko has assured me that the match was on the level, but the British press saw the static stances, and concluded (as usual incorrectly) that neither man was trying. So newspapers turned their reporting over to boxing, which, thanks to the incomparable Georges Carpentier, put the glove game into the headlines.

In 1929 this new style of wrestling had brought in fast, strong heavyweights like Jack Sherry, who possessed the stamina of long-distance runners. They had enormous endurance and were not only trained to a peak of muscular strength, but could stay any time limit in a competitive contest. In this way the elephants were overwhelmed by these tigers. Fast and good-looking Londos (then world champion) exemplified this style, as had Gus Sonnenberg, when he drew a record crowd to his championship match in Boston.

Many British journalists, knowing nothing about wrestling technique, mistook this wearing-down process for not trying, which was just about as sensible as saying that a competitor in the mile is not trying because he does not run off from the start at full speed, using his maximum powers! On the other hand, unless you are an expert it is obvious that this 'wearing down' process can also be used to fool the public. The contestants may not be trying at all, but putting on an acrobatic exhibition according to the instructions of their promoters, who have protected them from genuine challengers by the famous closed-shop motto: 'Right of admission strictly reserved.' Whereas,,,, to make a contest 'no one barred is a sure way of distinguishing between the competitive and the commercial.

A few weeks' training each day with this master matman and I showed an improvement beyond all imagination. Instead of being exhausted or beaten in the ten minutes of my amateur days I found I could stand up to the fast pace of this great heavyweight for an hour or more. In fact, on one occasion it took Karl two hours to beat me. At this time I was still 13 st g Ibs, the light-heavyweight limit in wrestling.

The idea came to me that I needed a sparring partner, or, as the Americans call it, a 'work-mate'. So I sent a ticket to Bulldog Bill Garnon of Fishguard, the seventeen stone heavyweight champion of Wales !

Bill's propensity for drinking enormous quantities of fizzy lemonade was well known to his friends. It so reduced the acidity of his body that he was never seasick. On his voyage, in the old four funnelled Mauretania, the seas were enormous. Except for a steward everyone else on board was sick. Bill came down to breakfast at the height of the storm and asked this steward, still on duty, 'What's for breakfast!' The poor man, handkerchief to mouth, shouted 'Take the bloody lot' and dashed out. Bill, who had a huge appetite, then ate the breakfast of this dreams with nothing barred. So much for fizzy drinks!

So Garnon arrived in New York. Nothing ever perturbed or upset him. Once, when asked what he thought of the view coming into New York he said, 'Not bad.' Alfred Pike suggested that he might like to help with weeding. (Alf ran a landscape gardening business.) 'Okay,' said Bill, 'where do I start?' It was a hundred in the shade and, later that morning, Alfred came in and said, 'That Garnon of yours is typically British. Just look at him.' I took a quick look, knowing exactly what to expect. Bill was lying full length on the grass pulling out weeds in slow motion and throwing them into a basket. I went over in a fair rage, and angrily said, 'When you come to a man's house and agree to help him in his garden you might make a little more effort. In fact you are like Luigi's dog.'

'Who was Luigi's dog;" asked Bill, half-asleep.

'Luigi's dog', I replied, 'was so lazy he had to lean against a wall to bark.'

'If I'd been Luigi's dog,' said Bill, 'I wouldn't have bothered to bark. When do we get tea?'

Whatever could be said for or against Garnon's energy when doing things which didn't interest him, no one could fault his wrestling. We wrestled for hours in all that heat, every morning, and every afternoon and again in the evening. Never, before or since, had I been so fit. My weight, thanks to buckets of ice-cream, baked salmon and rich American food, had at last risen to over fifteen stone, all muscle. My chest measured 52 in, my thighs 29 in, biceps 20 in and neck 22 in. I called Harry and we went to see Curley.

The expression on Curley's face when Harry and I walked in was something to remember. 'Say, Cap,' he said, 'that Pikey has sure been feeding you. You look in good shape too. Let's see what you go now.'

The scales showed two hundred and fifteen pounds. I was there. The next thing was to get a licence from the New York State Commission.

'If you'll call me Harry,' said Curley, 'I'll give you his first date!'

6. My American Tour: Casey Berger, the Texas Champ

A few days later Garsh came round to tell me that I was to appear at the 71st Armoury, one of the largest American stadiums after Madison Square Garden.

'Who against!' I asked.

'The Texas Champ. Oh boy, am I worried. It's a real tough assignment. Maybe we made a mistake letting Curley see you the other day. You sure look good now. I figure they're having second thoughts and taking no chances.'

So at last my great day arrived. Alfred drove Bill and me to the stadium. Pojello was already there looking more like a professor than ever. With his usual smile he said, (Atol, I think you give big Champion prescription. You believe what I say. Karl knows best. You take things steady. No rush. This man, big man. Very strong man. You no let him get grip or you finish upside down. You wait right time. Take great opportunity soon you see it. No try pin. Just grab foot. You try submission. I tell you. I know you listen. You win! You very big drawing card. Everyone come to see you. You will say, "Thank you, Mr. Pojello. You tell truth." You like very much Mr. Pojello.'

The main fight was for the world heavyweight championship between Ray Steele, a leading contender, and Jim Londos, Champion of Greece and reigning world champion. The stadium had been sold out for days.

Unlike the British journalists, American pressmen know how to write up wrestling, and wrestling here I found was very big business. A few weeks previously ninety thousand people had paid to see Gus Sonnenberg. Crowds of sixty thousand and more were commonplace. Wrestling had then completely eclipsed boxing, whose chief heavyweight and former wrestling champion, the Italian Primo Carnera, had failed to draw the paying customers on any great scale. This was due to his size, power and weight, which dwarfed his opponents. Boxing attendances were right down. The public do not pay to see a vast great man beating a small man. They like to see small men beat big men. So it has always been since the days of Goliath.

Primo Carnera, a giant 6 ft 7 in wrestler weighing nineteen stone, had invaded the sacred rights of the glove game and had, in his prime, easily demolished the lot, without knowing much about the art. He punched so hard that in training they made him wear 24 oz gloves. With ordinary boxing gloves he killed Schaaf. After this he lost his nerve. Primo was invincible as a glove fighter, as the world and America found out. But once he had killed a man Primo told me that he could no longer hit hard in case he killed anyone else. Thereafter, he said, he always pulled his punches. In due course he sank back into that oblivion which he enjoyed until Paul Joumee (for Jeff Dickson) found him wrestling all comers, fifteen a night, in France. But more about Carnera later.

Meantime I found myself in a large dressing room completely surrounded by huge men, muscled like gorillas, and about as big. Some were seven feet in height. The smallest, other than Londos the champion, measured at least six foot. I saw no one there except Londos who was anywhere near my size. The smallest of the giants was nineteen stone. Even the champion was of a much heavier build than I was.

Jack Pfeiffer, Curley's manager, came into the dressing room and told the preliminaries to get a move on. He came over to me and asked:

'Well, Cap, how you feel!'

I looked at Pfeiffer, who was around five foot eight and a hundred and twenty pounds. 'Pleased to find someone smaller than myself,' I replied: 'Okay, Jack, and could I be told which of these giants is Mr. Berger?' He said: 'You'll find out. You're not on till after the main bout anyway. See you later.'

When he returned to the dressing room Pfeiffer said: 'Now listen to me, Cap, we all admire you for coming all this way from little old England to do battle with our big boys. We have decided to give you a break. You're up against Casey Berger, Texas Champ. It's a thirty-minute match. We know how you paid your round-trip over and we've billed you real good.'

(He certainly had; 'Captain Atholl Oakeley, Scion of Kings', was my billing!)

'We don't aim to make you lose face at home so we're going to do you proud. Casey will give you a five-minute exhibition. After that we'll put up a card. Then you gotta do your best. This gives you five minutes' sure good chance to show yourself to the American public. After five minutes Casey aims to beat you right away because he is a great champion and he has his reputation to consider. You can go home and tell your folks you stayed five minutes against our champion.'

Good old Jack Pfeiffer ! I was deeply touched. Here was I in a foreign country, bombastically challenging men much bigger than I was. An Englishman at that, and the English, despite statements to the contrary, are usually much too stuck up to be really popular in the States. Here was a little American manager saying they did not wish to hurt me but, in their own way, try to enhance my reputation.

Irslinger, who had spent hours advising me in England as to what I might expect in America, had not prepared me for such generosity.

'Atol,' he had said, 'your heavyweights do not get enough experience in England to take on Americans in their own country. Your country produces great champions only in the lighter weights. Even if an English heavyweight was able to win over an American champ in America, or even looked like doing so, the ref would disqualify him.

'I figure, over in the States where there are 20,000 heavies, no English heavyweight is able to beat even their fourth raters. But maybe you can succeed. You have lots of experience against the best Europeans. You train a long time. You also got what it takes to make a champ—courage and speed.'

Perhaps Henri believed that I might have a chance in America because of my size and style. He had impressed upon me that their heavyweight wrestling champions at that time were men of great size and strength who, compared with me, would be slow and ponderous. Their strength made it imperative that at all costs I should avoid being caught in any grip from which I would be unable to escape.

Henri said that, being accustomed to fighting men of their own size, these giant champions from nations all over the world would think nothing of me. If I ever let them get a grip they would crush me.

This kind of talk, from so experienced a fighter as Henri Irslinger (remember he had won the open 'London Tournament' of 1908), had made me all the more determined to win.

But now I felt a small, rather insignificant little Englishman surrounded by giants in a foreign country. I did not even know which of these men was Casey Berger, my first opponent.

But I was not kept long in suspense. A good-looking Hercules came over and drawled, 'Hiya. I'm Berger. Casey Berger. Glad to know you, Cap.' He smiled, then ambled away with the measured gate of a Southerner. This then was Casey Berger. He looked all that Karl had said he was.

I continued thinking:

'This is a strong and determined man. I must not be fooled by that smile. Casey is not going to take any chances against a little fifteen-stoner. My only chance of winning will be speed and a ferocious attack—as rough as possible, a l'Irslinger, and right from the start. I must show him I am no pushover.'

I remembered how I had blacked the eye of world champion Svediquist in the final of the championships in Brussels three years previously. The American press regarded all Englishmen as (outwardly) over-polite and (inwardly) perfidious. Casey would not expect rough tactics. More likely, as I later heard, he expected me to follow the usual pattern. Namely retiring with a cut eye or flinging myself horizontal, holding my steel protector-cap and screaming 'foul' at the top of my voice.

It may well have been that the Texas champion took me too lightly. In view of performances by other British heavyweights, who had ventured into the lion's den of the American ring, one could hardly blame him.

I awoke from my day dreams with a bang.

'You're on now, Cap. Get goin',' called out Jack Pfeiffer. As I: passed him, wearing my black and white silk dressing gown, skin-tight black tights trimmed with chocolate and gold (my regimental Athletic Team colours), he said:

'Say, you look all right. I hope they hoovered the mat for you, Cap.

Then he saw my knee-pads:

'What you aim to do—play cricket!'

As I walked up the aisle I heard people saying:

'This is the English aristocrat. My, but he looks a smart little fellow.

'Surely they're not Putting that little guy on with Berger. He'll get killed.'

'Heard he came over from England just to challenge us.' 'Yes, I hoid all that befoire. Last Big British Palooka ended up on his back yelling foul.'

Someone else replied: 'That little fellow won't get a chance to yell foul.'

Then suddenly an English voice called out:

'Come on, England. We're all rooting for you to show these Yanks where they get off. Rule, Britannia, old boy, and don't bloody well forget it!'

That effort clinched it! I would beat this Texan or never again enter a wrestling ring! I climbed up the steps, vaulted the ropes and went over to my corner.

My appearance was greeted with one big howl of laughter. I bowed sedately and was greeted, if possible, by even louder laughter. There were shouts of, 'This game ought to suit British heavyweights. Why don't you lie down like the rest of your champions! You look more natural horizontal!'

'You English send your Prince of Wales to South America. You, son of a bitch, they send to us.

'How long before your eye opens up, Cap!'

Casey followed me in at a slow pace, and stepped nonchalantly over the top rope. He bowed slightly to the crowd and ignored me.

He got a terrific reception. Texans are very popular in the States, as well they might be. Casey Berger was a great drawing card, and rightly thought much of by the American sporting public.

'Hey, Casey', I heard someone call, 'why you put on against welterweights! What happened to all the heavies!'

The referee followed Casey. I at once recognised Gunboat Smith —one of the most famous of all boxers. One who knew ring fighters, of both fight games, from A to Z. A professional who had forgotten more than all the ex-amateur heavyweights of later generations ever knew.

The announcer, Mr. Humphries (who wore a hat), said, 'ladies and gentlemen. It gives me pleasure to present Captain Atholl Oakeley, Champion of England, who has come to our shores to make good his challenge to beat our champions. Give the Captain a hand.'

There was some polite clapping.

'And in this corner Casey Berger whom you all know. Uproar again for their idol.

'Hiya, Casey. Do your stuff, boy, I heard someone shout.' Casey's face remained a mask.

We went to our corners and took off our dressing gowns—or robes' as the Americans call them.

I walked to the centre of the ring and held out my hand. Casey brushed it aside and got booed.

Without more ado I stepped in, grabbed a headlock and buttocked him. All his nineteen stone went crashing to the mat. The Texan pulled loose and stood up. He walked crabwise across the ring and stood in a corner.

Someone called out, 'Two minutes.'

Casey came out of the corner bulling in the initial headhold then using brute force to bring me to my knees. Changing to a half nelson he levered me onto my shoulders and held me. I raised one shoulder clear, thus 'stopping' a fall with the bent leg check as taught us at the Ashdown. Casey seemed puzzled at this. (Four minutes,) called the timekeeper.

One minute to go. I stayed, held as in a vice. This man was not only heavy; he was much stronger than anyone I had met before. I would have to keep clear. I thought, 'If I let this big chap get a firm hold on me I'm done for.'

Casey slacked the half nelson. I rolled on my stomach, knelt up, shot my legs forward into a sitting position, turned to my left and stood up.

'Five minutes.'

I suddenly saw, mat level, Casey's chief second hold a card towards me. On it was written:

'You're on your own Cap.'

Casey glanced casually towards his corner and like a flash I was on him. All the best Irslinger tactics! Three hard forearms, left, right, left, I put into his face, then, double wrist-locking him, I brought him to the mat before he realised what was going on. Neck scissors (he broke it) followed by a straight scissors and face bar. His nose bled.

'First blood to me,' I thought. 'So far so good.' I hauled his head back and heard his neck creak.

Casey, by this time, was acting like an infuriated bull. He broke the scissors, throwing me off and storming to his feet.

We had a furious fist fight in a corner. Our four seconds and the referee intervened to separate us.

'Son of a bitch,' growled Berger to the ref. 'What the hell is this, a wrestling match or a god damned prize fight?'

'Cap,' says the ref, 'I don't go for rough tactics. Quit all that bare knuckle stuff or out you go. Now fight on.'

Casey, really roused, threw me with a 'supplice'. I grabbed the bottom rope and hauled myself out of the ring. I fell on the floor with a bang. Re-entering the ring I ran into an American flying mare and got shot out of the ring the other side. This time I knocked over an elderly man wearing glasses. Again I got back into the ring. ('Nine minutes,' called the timekeeper.) 'Cap's greasy,' said Casey to the ref.

Gunboat Smith called for a towel and dried 'What you got on! Looks like grease to me.

'Sure slippery, says the Texan. 'I can't hold him. Get him dried.' The referee dried me again with some force.

'Okay now. Fight on!'

The next five minutes was a real tear-up. Casey grabbed every hold in the book but so slippery was I that he failed to hold me. The more he tried and failed the more furious he became. I felt his strength was so great that only counter-moves, and slips, executed with great speed, could save me.

I nearly got caught with a chancery and bar; then by a figure four scissors, then in a short arm scissors, and finally a Further Nelson. I managed to escape from all these-the last one by 'spinning'.

Casey, now really angry at sarcastic shouts from the crowd who were beginning to get excited and vociferous, went back into the initial head hold and bulled me into a corner, where he forced a crotch hold and body-slammed me very hard indeed.

Somewhat winded by the force of the impact I managed to slip free and so under the ropes.

Minute after minute this went on with Casey furiously trying to hold me, while time and again I slipped free.

By the time the twenty-fourth minute was called the whole arena was in a pandemonium. The noise was ear-splitting, one gigantic deafening roar nearly breaking my ear drums. Hundreds of people were jumping up and down in their seats, all bawling at Casey who replied by again picking me up and slamming me, then throwing himself onto me in a desperate effort to get the fall. With one shoulder down I screwed my hips round and slipped out of his clutches.

Then it was that I saw the card which sent me hopping mad: 'Okay Casey go for a draw.'

As I say, this card so infuriated me that all the hereditary instincts of my prize-fighting grandfather came welling up inside me. I knew then it was a case of 'do or die', and that everything rested on one fast and bold move.

Having returned once again from my usual escape-exit under the ropes I saw this giant of a man standing, legs apart, his great hands on his hips, waiting for me.

'This,' I remember thinking, 'Is Kyburz all over again.' I knew what I was going to get. In a flashback I saw myself once more in hospital just as I was after that terrible body slam at the Salle Wagram in Paris, when referee Davis saw World Champion Kyburz raise the dust sky high as, from high overhead, he crashed me to the canvas, into oblivion and hospital.

With all my waning strength and speed, I catapulted myself between and through the Texan's legs. Berger must have wondered where I had gone to!

Then like a swimmer at the turn, as quick as lightning, I twisted round, locking one of this ankles with my left arm, one with my right. I hauled in my shoulders against his huge calves, I felt like a maniac. Would Casey fall! For a moment he stood. Then, like a falling tree, this colossal Texan Champion shivered, and crashed full length to the canvas. . . !

I whipped up both legs, stepped over them and barred his mouth, savagely digging in my knuckles and straining his head7back. Still this steelman did not tap. I pulled my bare knuckles up under his nose which was already streaming blood.

I leant forward till I felt his knee joint creak. Casey, most gallant of all men, only groaned but still did not submit. A minute ticked by. I released the face lock and concentrated on the leg lock. The noise in the stadium was absolutely deafening. The sound seemed as if all the devils in hell had been let loose. Still Casey would not submit. It became fantastic, unreal, like a dream. The din grew even worse.

Blood and sweat poured from Casey's face, now deathly white. I remembered Irslinger's final advice.

'If they won't submit, frighten them.'

But how could one frighten this Texan? Nothing ever frightens these Texans.

Casey just wasn't the type to be frightened. As a man he was superb, his courage was magnificent. He was caught and he knew it, but he would never surrender. What a man!

Desperately I turned my back on the ref and deliberately twisted one foot, with a circular movement, against the ankle joint: one of the sinister moves taught me by Irslinger. Determined to remember the lesson of Phil Scott and others I knew I had to win this fight.

Casey, furious and now in dire agony, pointed to his foot. The referee bawled 'Stop that, Cap.' But his voice sounded miles away. It all seemed utterly unreal, I felt as if in a dream.

The twenty-fifth minute came up.

I forced my knuckles under Berger's arm-pits and I thrust them through, grinding them down so taking double arm locks.

With both legs napped in step-over toe holds and both arms drawn right up his back with double arm locks into barred hammer locks the Texan could not move one single inch in any direction.

In another 35 seconds, as I increased to full pressure, he tapped. I heard someone yell, 'My God he's beaten him!'

It took the seconds, his and mine, helped by the referee, at least another two minutes to unravel us, so interlocked were our legs. I think I must have fainted.

The next thing I remember was someone lifting me, like a corpse, clear over the ropes. People grabbed me. Some man had me on his shoulder and was carrying me out. All around a sea of faces, a surging milling crowd, buffeted us. I remember thinking, 'If this was a hostile crowd I would certainly be lynched.'

But they were not hostile. Their champion had fallen but, like our British crowds, they were grand sportsmen. David had slain Goliath.

That is what fight crowds all over the world go mad to see and have done since time immemorial.

Men were shouting 'Well done, little guy—guess you got what it takes', and 'The King will sure be proud of you'.

But the King was not proud of me. He never knew, because the British press suppressed all reference to the fight.

7. A Limey's Progress Through the States

The following morning, bruised all over and with two black eyes, I awoke to find Alfred standing beside the bed holding a huge bundle of papers.

To quote from all the write-ups might savour of conceit. Anyway it would take too long, but there were some amusing touches. In one paper, for instance, there was a large picture of me holding Casey in a splits. Underneath they put: 'Oh Captain how could you?' Another account was captioned: 'Oakeley looks good in New York Bow', and underneath the Sports Editors wrote:

'Captain Atholl Oakeley downed Texas Champ Casey Berger in 25 mins 35 secs with a body spread and double arm lock. The British champion made a fine impression though his weight is going to be a handicap. He had to use all that was in him to get his man in the end. The Captain flopped Casey to the floor almost immediately as they got of the mark. A headlock brought Berger to the floor and, after a few minutes, Berger pulled out and they came afoot again. The Captain was held in a Half Nelson and broke away. He got as rough as you please and Gunboat Smith, a gentle lamb of athletics, shook a warning finger under the Englishman's nose. Once, when the British boy used a free foot to bring Berger's head close to the floor, the crowd protested with the gunner. He is a slippery individual is the Briton. He obtained a toe hold, on two occasions, which made Berger pull faces which would have frightened Stasjak of the Out- Oakeley wore heavy rubber knee pads and looked like a cricket player.

'Berger was stronger than Oakeley and used this power to punish the visitor every time he got an opportunity.

Under a picture of Casey in mid air, Randolph Hearst's Daily News wrote:

Blimey! If they don't wrestle better than they box-fight in jolly old London. Captain Atholl Oakeley, seen tossing Casey Berger over his shoulder, proved it to the fans last night when he stopped Casey Berger with a double arm and body lock.'

Another national daily gave this account:

Captain Atholl Oakeley defeated "Roughhouse" Casey Berger in a bout in which was exhibited many of the new holds which make the grappling game a sport which calls for the gamest kind of courage. :Captain Oakeley was the society idol of Great Britain, where his position is secure by being the nephew of Sir Charles Oakeley and in of the Duke of Atholl. He possesses a splendid physique, is an aristocrat in appearance and is in the wrestling game for the love of the sport. He holds the championship of Great Britain.'

The other American newspapers carried similar stories. But British newspapers not one line.

Later the Mirror admitted: 'News of Atholl Oakeley's successful debut in the States came through simultaneously with the result of Berg's defeat by Canzoneri, and his win over Kiser on points ten rounds.'

We never found a line in any other British newspaper.

The reason might well have been that which was printed by the or: 'I don't like the game AND I HOPE IT DOES NOT CATCH ON OVER HERE. But I have admiration for a brave man. So here's luck, Oakeley.

The widespread publicity afforded me by the wonderful American press was staggering. I had been accustomed to newspapers at home constantly and drearily bleating about the 'freedom of the press', while themselves unwilling to allow the freedom of their news columns to an event reported by newspapers throughout the world (even China!). I had therefore expected nothing at all in America. In particular Randolph Hearst was well known to have no time for the British. This alone makes the unbiased reporting of the American newsmen such a contrast to those at home. Even more staggering was the personal invitation sent me, by Mrs. Randolph Hearst, to fight on her world-famous 'Milk Fund' programme at the Yankee Stadium. An athletic honour granted only to the world's greatest fighters. The Welshman, Tommy Farr, is the only British heavyweight champion to be afforded such an honour. But my invitation made no mention of a title match with Londos.

Pojello and Garsh felt I needed a rest to recover from my bruises and lick my wounds. Offers began to pour in from all over America and South America but Curley decided I was, for the time being at any rate, to fight only in New York. Next he chose Zelezniak the Russian.

In world championship boxing and wrestling it was not unusual for some so-called champions to be 'protected' from world challengers. Some promoters insisted that dangerous challengers, who seemed likely to defeat the champion, should fist fight a 'Policeman.'

This was a super-strong fighter, nearly always coloured, and of great size and strength. To be made to fight one of these men was in itself a compliment since second-raters were invariably matched straight against current world champions without first having to meet his Policeman.

The usual practice was for the coloured man, under penalty of being shot by gangsters, to go down for his lighter opponent. But sometimes the latter got in such a tiz that he fumbled the knockout. Or the coloured fighter was such a bad actor that, to the experts, he gave the game away by retiring hurt or going down and out to a blow, ill put over, which would not hurt a child. I found people in the professional fight game knew all about this. It was no myth.

One of my friends was told to lose to a so-called wrestling 'champion of the world'. To get the match he agreed. Then he told the good-looking 'champion' to do his best and beat him in 18 minutes.

The following morning his wife's car was forced off a mountain road. She fell zoo feet and was killed. When the car was found, pinned to what was left of her was a note: 'Next time do as you're told.'

While no one ever asked me to lose, this was probably because no one but a lunatic expected me to win. However, before the Casey fight the New York Gang did ask me for ten per cent. Bill Garnon and I were on good terms with Schultz so we paid up. You can't win over organised gangsters!

My old friend Stanislaus Zbyszko (who was a leading figure in American wrestling) called to see me. He said my defeat of Berger had taken everyone by surprise and that the public were clamouring for a match with Londos. It appeared my style was different to what the leaders were accustomed to. This, coupled with my speed and slipperiness, was causing the big men some concern.

He warned me that I was to be matched against the colossal Zelezniak, then the heavyweight champion of Russia. He said I had no chance whatever and could not possibly give away so much weight. The idea was obviously to 'bump me off' (speaking in fight parlance) and send me back to England.

Zbyszko was no fool. He had been active in wrestling ever since the days of Hackenxhmidt, well before the Great V(War of 1914. I had no doubt he was telling me the truth and was genuinely concerned for me. He emphasised over and over again that Zelezniak was a very different proposition to Irslinger or Boganski. No one had beaten him for some years and he was fighting all comers at the rate of one a week.

Garsh did not like the match either. Finally Pojello joined in. 'Atol you no meet Vanka yet—I know this man. He great Russian wrestler. He very strong, very experienced. You ask first smaller man. You lucky beat Casey—next time maybe you not so lucky.'

I wondered whether I should sign the contract, but not to have done so would have made nonsense of my boastful challenge. So, not without grave misgivings, I signed.

The match was to take place in New York and I began more intensive training than ever before. Under the tropical sun, with temperatures over 100 in the shade, Bill Garnon and I wrestled for hours each day. By drinking huge quantities of water, eating ice cream (by the bucket!) my weight remained steady at 215 lbs.

So my second great day came. In the dressing room Zelezniak looked me up and down and spat on the floor. Steinke, who was on before me, gave me his money wrapped up and tied in a handkerchief. 'You hold this, mein frewnd! Dankerschan.' When he came back I found I had lost it. I had visions of being held outside the window. Eventually I found the handkerchief in my other pocket.

But the scare did not help my equilibrium.

Zelezniak and I were the main fight on the case. He went into the ring first. When I appeared there was a gasp of amazement. Then uproarious laughter with shouts of, 'What's this, a joke? Give us our money back.' The situation became ugly and the police came in. It took some time before the crowd would listen to the announcer.

From my fights with George Boganski, I knew only too well how callous these Russians can be and I was in a real sweat. Most awkward too because the olive oil, with which Bill had massaged me, was coming out prematurely! I had not forgotten how Boganski had tied me up in a shorearm scissors and then smashed his clenched fist, time and time again, into the pit of my stomach. The American press had represented me as an aristocrat and this also annoyed the Russian. I had no doubt at all as to what I had let myself in for. His very appearance was appalling, and he made it even worse with frightful grimaces. If Casey Berger had been formidable, this huge gorilla was fantastic. Garsh, Bill and Alfred were all looking worried.

They told me after that they never expected me to come out alive. Pojello had refused to attend at all, so certain was he that this was my last match.

Even the sports editors thought the fight ridiculous. The New York Herald wrote, apropos my challenge for the world heavyweight title:

'Captain Atholl Oakeley, the British Champion, is here to challenge Londos should he win over Vanka Zelezniak the Russian. If the Captain is good enough to challenge Londos he should be able to dispose of anybody standing in the way.

That 'anybody' being Vanka Zelezniak!

The referee said, 'Shake hands.' Zelezniak looked at the audience, then at me, spat on the floor. The referee went on:

'You know the rules. No strangles, no palm-up flying mares, and no barred hammer lock. And, Cap, this time no hitting with your fists. Now go to your corners. Come out fighting and may the best man win.' Then to me, 'Watch your step, young fellow. We don't want no accidents.'

I came out and, following my usual practice, jumped up four or five feet and clamped on my leg-headlock. Zelezniak pulled me off his neck like you might pull off a rat. The next moment I arrived on the lap of a fat man in the fourth row. The chair broke, we landed on the floor, and I collided with a man and a woman in the fifth row who then joined the floor party. Such a schemozzle! Two men helped me back to the ringside. No sooner had I got in, than Zelezniak picked me up and threw me out. Again my fall was broken.

By this time hopping mad, I moved into a corner. Zelezniak came over. I hooked both arms over the top rope and both legs round the lower rope. He tried to pull me loose. His face was a foot away so I suddenly drove in my right hand. Bare fist hitting is not as easy as you might think. One usually hurts oneself or breaks the metacarpal bones. But I had been taught pugilism by the former prize fighter 'Dynamite' Shaw and my hands had been pickled with sheep's gall and alum which the 'Fancy' used in the olden days.

The effect was magical. Vanka went down as if he had been pole-axed. I followed him down and clamped on a scissors round his neck. The referee tried to disqualify me but the audience were kicking up such a noise that no one could hear and I didn't want to. In any case nothing would have made me relinquish my hold for fear of being thrown right out of the hall. Zelezniak, now in a real rage, was struggling like a wounded bull.

Eventually he got free. He stood up, towering over me. His attack began, slow and ponderous. Much faster, I eluded his holds. As in the Casey Berger fight, now that I was hot Zelezniak could not hold me. Accustomed to fighting much bigger men, his hands slipped off every hold. Time and time again the referee had me dried. Vaseline was now coming out of every pore. Zelezniak's eye was closed. A trickle of blood ran down his cheek. Twice I got short-arm scissors but each time he stood up and threw me off. Then he made the same mistake as Casey. Standing, with his hands on his hips, legs apart, he glowered at me. Like a flash I was through his legs and down he crashed, with his foot doubled up his back and with a double arm-locked hammer lock to assist it. No one, except the great Jack Sherry, could have escaped from this combination of holds. Trussed like a chicken, he gave in at the nineteenth minute. So my way was clear for Londos. Garsh was nearly in tears. Garnon had to revive himself with bottles of fizzy lemonade. But the uproar which had followed the Berger fight was absent. The American crowd seemed stunned. There was an eerie silence which you could almost feel. A year later Vanka Zelezniak won the heavyweight championship of the world in Buenos Aires.

I never saw him again. Karl came over next day. 'Atol, I make you greatest wrestler. These boys no understand your style. You so fast they no catch you like they catch bigger men. But Londos different. He faster and stronger than you. I know. I figure they not let you wrestle Londos anyway. You get frame-up. You see. Karl right.'

My next opponent was the famous Omaha Champion, Jack Burke. He was reputed to be very fast, but was not much bigger than me. The promoters had changed their tactics: no colossus this time but a really fast and courageous heavyweight. Here I met the famous flying tackle for the first time. Jack went backwards onto the top rope. He forced it out towards the audience, and it snapped him back like a catapult. I ducked, only just in time. Burke sailed over my head, right over the top rope behind me and into the audience. But he came back, fighting furiously, and in the tenth minute he again tried his flying: tackle. I stood up under him as he shot over, so somersaulting him. He fell upside down and had to retire, rather badly cut and hurt. This was never my intention, but the force with which he went over me was far greater than I realised. Intending to grab his ankle, my shoulder caught his thighs. Glad I am to say that he made a complete recovery and I offered him my apologies. No one deliberately injures a person in wrestling. Men are injured by accident or by illogically refusing to give in when trapped.

In boxing you cannot give in, unless the referee stops your fight. Undefended head punches cause serious brain damage resulting in punch-drunkenness—a condition never found in any wrestler. In wrestling-competitive wrestling—it is no disgrace to give in. In fact, with holds like the Boston crab, crooked head scissors and Japanese leg lock, you must give in. I am of course not referring to exhibition wrestling where the acrobats escape with the greatest of ease from every hold, like the man on the flying trapeze. I can assure you, dear reader, no man born can escape from these locks unless he is allowed to. Nor can you throw a man into a somersault by jerking his wrist. These are fine action studies calculated to thrill the uninitiated. But the national amateur wrestling champions of Britain will tell you that these holds are just baloney. If anyone living could have thrown me by jerking my wrist I would have retired on the spot and recommended him to David Devant's theatre of magic.

Having now won three matches off the reel I was matched with former Olympic Champion George Tragos of Greece, the best heavyweight from Greece after Londos. Here again was a man of my own size and weight. He had developed, as I had, from lighter divisions. Olympic champions, past or present, cannot be taken lightly as the promoters well knew. This was an ex-amateur chosen because he would know my basic style. I have no hesitation in admitting, had I met this great wrestler before Pojello took me in hand, he would have easily beaten me. Considerably heavier than Irslinger or Bognnski, Tragos was very fast indeed. He used chain holds in bewildering succession. Rightly or wrongly I got the impression that Londos himself arranged this match in the belief that his countryman, through his great speed in chain holds, would succeed where others had failed.

The match was a wrestling classic, fast, clean and furious. I used no grease against a man of my own weight. The speed of Tragos was all it was cracked up to be. He put standing double wrist locks on with such speed and force that I was hard pressed to go with them.

(To have resisted would have resulted in my shoulder being dislocated.) But not withstanding his great speed and long experience, Tragos failed to beat me. My youth, strength, stamina and perfect training alone turned the table against this older, more experienced and highly scientific matman. I have no doubt but that George Mackenzie and Vic Benson (my tutors during my young amateur days) would have called this my finest hour. To win by skill alone and without aids against a man of such ability was the aim instilled in me by all at the old Ashdown Club in Islington. I felt that Jack Davis, Mackenzie, Vic, and World Champion Stan Bacon would have been proud of their pupil. In all modesty the victory over Tragos was my best ever.

Having now defeated the main opposition I expected a world championship match. Instead I was sent to Canada to meet champion Louis Lachine. I beat him before a huge crowd in the arena of the Queensbury Athletic Club in Toronto, and followed this up with another victory, at Montreal, against the Jewish champion Benny Ginsberg, in 25 minutes. I engaged in two other fights, both of which I won, before setting off to return to America. In the eyes of the public I was now a star attraction.

On my last night in Montreal the team of wrestlers from USA went out to celebrate their victories over the Canadians. When I returned from a movie the hotel porter said, 'You's better look in Room — and see your buddies.' Knocking brought no reply so I opened the door and went in. There were our team members, piled up seven deep on a bed (which had given way): Romano at the bottom, Abe Caplan (wearing a baseball cap) on top.

The next morning I roused them (not without difficulty) and went off to catch the train. There was no sign of anyone on the platform. and the train pulled out. At the next station it stopped. There, getting out of a taxi, was our team.

Before we reached the American border they had a conference as to how they could get their whisky and cigarettes past the Customs. (There was Prohibition, remember.) The majority vote was adopted that the parcels should be wrapped and put in the luggage rack. 'Leave them just natural,' observed someone, 'and no one's goin' to get curious.'

'You guys can leave your booze there if you like,' said Abe Caplan, 'but I don't aim to lose my bottle.' And he went out into the corridor. The Customs came around.

'Anything to declare!' Our great tough men looked the picture of innocence. The Customs glanced round and left.

Shortly afterwards Abe strolled out and returned furious. 'What the hell. Look at this.'

He held up the telephone directory which had been chained to a desk in the corridor. He opened the book. He had cut out the centre of the pages into the shape of a halfbotte. But the bottle, so carefully concealed, had gone!

Back in the States the train stopped and a young, good-looking, travelling salesman came into our compartment.

'Mornin' folks,' he said. 'You look like wrestlers.'

'We is,' grunted Caplan. 'Want to make something of it?'

(No sir, sure don't.' He looked around.

'Any of you guys interested in these?'

He opened a suitcase full of ties.

'I've got to get rid of this bunch before I get to New York. You see I've been on Lake George with a dame. If I go back with this lot I'll get fired.'

The ties were silk and obviously expensive. 'Give you a dime for this one,' said Caplan.

'It's yours,' says the salesman.

Everyone woke up. At a dime apiece he sold us his whole stock of about a hundred ties!

Mike Romano, the Italian champion, whiled the time away by telling me a story which well illustrates the fallacy that world champion boxers or wrestlers are necessarily the best in the world. Just as Miss World is not necessarily the most beautiful girl. There are people who never appear before the general public, but who could in certain circumstances make most promoted champions look small fry.

Now Mike was one of the top ten wrestlers in the States. He was a great heavyweight, equal to Berger or even Zelezniak.

Some years before, he told me, he and three other American heavyweights had been barnstorming. They stayed a week in each town. At night these four took on all comers. $100 for beating No. 4, $200 for beating No. 3, $500 for beating No. 2 and $1000 for beating Mike himself. No one was barred and half-fees were paid to anyone staying ten minutes. The general idea was to match whoever lasted longest during the week in a fight to the fight against Romano on Saturday night. This always attracted a large crowd.

Of course, no one had stood up very long to Romano. That was until the team got to a small town in Texas.

There, on the Wednesday night, a Texan cowboy standing seven feet high, famous in the town for his strength and courage, pinned No. 4 in a minute. This he did by picking him up and falling on him.

On the Thursday night he threw the next two in a minute each. On the Friday night he elected to try for the prize offered to anyone staying ten minutes with No. I wrestler, Mike Romano.

Mike said the idea in this was that he had to try to throw the Texan but the latter had only to avoid being thrown. If he succeeded in staying the distance the challenger would receive $500 and a match to the finish on the Saturday night.

In the ten-minute match Romano took the initial hold and, by sheer force, was thrown flat on his face in the first second. He got to his feet. 'Sure was real shaken,' he said. 'It was like holding onto a steel girder. I could not move him nor bend him a fraction of an inch. He just stood there and broke every hold I tried to get. I tried everything I knew.

Ten minutes elapsed and the Texas giant got his $500? The group tried to talk him out of the Saturday night match.

'The Texan,' Mike said, 'just drawled he wanted to take the match to a finish. I told him okay, but I knew I couldn't last a minute. 'What on earth did you do!' I asked.

'Well, I'll tell you,' said Romano.

'On Saturday night my three partners gave their usual exhibitions. The giant arrived at the theatre. We took him up to the top dressing room and told him to get ready. When the time came for him to wrestle we sent someone up to tell him. But our guy didn't tell him. He locked him in. That afternoon we had replaced the lock with one much stronger. The door was oak. No one could break that down.' Romano went on:

'I came onto the stage and waited five minutes. Meantime there was loud banging going on so we got the orchestra to play loud music. After ten minutes the announcer said, "Ladies and gentlemen. Mr. Romano is here ready to wrestle but where is your man!"

'After another ten minutes the audience got their money back and went home. We got dressed and the hammering on the door was terrible. None of us dared to let him out. We couldn't leave him there all night. So we had a whip round and gave a hundred bucks and the key to the page boy, with instructions he was only to unlock the door after we were on our train and it had left the durned town.' 'What happened then?' I asked.

'Well,' said Romano, 'a couple of years later we met one of the theatre attendants. He said the page boy had unlocked the door, which opened outwards, and quickly got close to the wall. The Texan flung open the door and rushed out like a madman. All night he was looking for us. In the morning he told everyone his version but no one believed him. Ever since all the little boys had shouted at him, 'Watch out, big cowboy, Romano's coming!'

So we arrived back in New York, complete with our ties. I had fifteen! The Canadian tour had been a great success for all of us, and our pockets were stuffed full of money. I had won all my matches. Like the American champions the Canadians could not figure out my Anglo-American style. Unlike the Americans the Canadians were not so strong as I was], though their courage was of course indisputable. I rated their average wrestling ability a little higher than that of the leading British amateurs of the day, but rather less than that of champions like William Templeton of Scotland, Douglas Clark of Huddersfield, and Jack Robinson of Newcastle. These men were the leading British professionals in the 'European Catch-as-Catch-Can' and 'Cumberland and Westmorland' styles at the time when Irslinger and I introduced the American Catch-as-Catch-Can to Britain in 1930.

Curley was delighted with the success of the tour. He showed me letters, from the Canadian promoters, asking why he had not sent over a British heavyweight wrestler before. Letter after letter came in with offers for matches all over Canada.

But I was not interested in any offers. All I wanted was the world championship fight with Jim Londos. Next day at Bothner's I said to Pojello:

'Karl, I am being side-stepped. Harry says that Ray Steele has been chosen for the title match at the Milk Fund. Is this true?'

'Atol, what I tell you. You now too dangerous. No promoter here permit English fighter take away heavyweight crown. Boxing or wrestling. Until you start show them different, American people here figure all your heavies bums. You also bum heavyweight till I teach you. Now you Pojello man. You learn plenty here with Karl. You go places. But best forget Londos. You go home now you beat everyone. Maybe you be European champ. You listen to Karl.'

Just as Pojello said, Jim Londos seemed to elude me. Try as I would I could not get the match. Later, much later, when Londos came to London to meet South African champion Van der Walt at the Royal Albert Hall, Jack Sherry followed him over here. We put ten thousand pamphlets outside the Albert Hall saying he would beat him within half an hour. At the time Londos was not world champion, and Sherry was. But the Greek champion would not wrestle the challenge. Nor did he ever take up mine in spite of my defeat of Vanka Zelemiak.

I had got so far in the States, but Londos did not appear to want to know. Or if he did the promoters would not, or could not, match us.

Thus the match for which I came, the world heavyweight championship, never materialised. Pojello said that they never intended it should, nor did they ever expect me to beat Berger, let alone Zelemiak.

8. Seventeen Victories on the Trot - Then Disappointment

On my return from Canada I accepted a challenge from George Hill, who had been a lumberjack in Wisconsin. This fight took place at Carlin's Park, Baltimore. Hill was known to be a man of considerable strength, as one would imagine from his profession. Pictures showed he had a wonderful physique. Remembering Mike Romano's story of the Texan Hercules I immediately began more intensive training with Bill Garnon, coupled with long hours of tuition from Karl Pojello.

Baltimore is about two hundred miles from New York. Pfeiffer handed me a round trip ticket and told me to be at Carlin's by 6 pm. I caught the fast train (and in America fast trains are really fast) as stated.

Hill was all he was cracked up to be. He was also a 'regular guy', as the Americans call popular people. After the match, which I won, we had supper together. He told me stories of his life as a lumberjack. 'Cap, if you wanta get washboard stomach muscles you just come along to the camp. You sure do get some strength swingin' axes all day. You swing an axe, Cap?'

'Not very well,' I replied. 'We once asked our forestry boss in England if three or four wrestlers could do some work for him and got a rude reply.'

'Guess you didn't have a card,' said Hill.

George was typical of the young Americans, whom I found to be manly, upright, courteous and full of humour. I liked them all immensely. American colleges like Oklahoma and Notre Dame specialise in wrestling and turn out many good athletes. There are ample gymnasiums in the States where anyone can train. It is the country of the young. England the country of the old. George Hill, a sportsman to his fingertips, personified all that was best in American sport.

After these nine victories I won another eight, so bringing my total victories off the reel in America and Canada to seventeen. By this time the American public, curious to see an English wrestling champion, and fired by all the publicity, were coming to my fights in increasing numbers. This of course pleased the promoters.

Every morning Pojello taught me. We worked three hours on standing throws and one hour on ground locks. Then half an hour running, and back to Pike's I went for lunch. At 3 pm Bill and I wrestled on carpets on Alfred's lawn. At 7 pm I bathed and was rubbed down with embrocation. At 8 pm dinner and at 10 pm to bed.

Such rigorous training brought me up to the highest pitch of physical perfection. Pojello would not allow me to swim or work with weights. He considered weight lifting (or, rather, exercises with heavy weights) only to be necessary for young people who wanted to build up their bodies. (Atol; chain no stronger than weak link-mat game only sport which builds strong neck.'

By this time I had learned Karl's style and could invariably stand up to him for forty minutes, having learned his holds and locks. Unfortunately, as it turned out later, Pojello knew all mine too. This man was not only a great wrestler but also a great coach. No one in England could live with him for more than a few minutes. Some leading British heavyweights were much too wise to say. The only wrestlers able to pin Karl were Jack Sherry and Hans Steinke. That was the calibre of this man.

Jack Curley was the official promoter for the Randolph Hearst Milk Fund programme.

He had written:

'For the first time in thirty-seven years I take pleasure to present to you a championship wrestler of great merit who is a member of the British nobility. Capt Atholl Oakeley is the finest looking prospect for championship honours and has come to our shores in quest of a championship match. He has won his spurs, has great personality and looks the part of a determined typical Britisher. Capt Atholl is a cousin of the Duke of Atholl and nephew of Sir Charles Oakeley, Bart. He served in the British Army and won his letters in one of the famous British Universities [a reference to the RMC, Sandhurst]. Burkes Peerage will give you more detailed information on this great athlete who is elevating the wrestling game by his able participation. Next to this was a large picture.

Hundreds of thousands of these pamphlets were sent out all over America.

It needed over sixty thousand people to fill the Yankee Stadium and most newspapers in America carried a full-page wrestling picture of one sort or another. The immense publicity provided in all their newspapers by the sponsors, the Hearst Press, ensured the success of the Milk Fund. This, as its name implied, was to Provide milk for

American babies. Only the world's leading fighters, nearly all of them heavyweights, are invited to fight on the Milk Fund programme.

Such an invitation is to fighters what an Oscar is to film stars. Wrestlers from all over the world and of all nationalities are featured in championship matches or championship eliminators. The main fight was the world heavyweight title match between Jim Londos, Champion of Greece and the world, and American champion Ray Steele.

In support were:

Babe Caddock	Vanka Zelezniak
v.	v.
Atholl Oakeley	Hans Kaempfer
v.	v.
Hans Steinke	Mike Romano
v.	v.
Dick Shikat	Herbee Freeman
Wladek Zbyszko	Sergei Kalmikoff
v.	v.
Carl Lemmle	Earl McCready

and other champions.

Afterwards the newspapers announced:

'Never in the history of New York has such a vast crowd been seen at a wrestling match.'

61,500 people paid for admission—more than at the GotchHackenschmidt match. In fact 40,000 more than the British indoor all-time record attendance at the Jack Doyle v. Eddie Phillips match at Earls Court Stadium in 1938.

These people were piled, tier upon tier, right over the ring. If you can imagine a crowd at an international rugger or football match which, instead of being spread out round the field, has all been compressed into a colossal soup bowl round a 24 foot ring, well, that was what the Yankee Stadium looked like that day so long ago.

Just to have the honour of being invited to appear at such a gathering of champions was an unforgettable experience. It was

Sir Atholl Oakeley, Bart., the author

also a shattering one for me because, as you will hear, I was held to have lost the match!

'Oh!' I hear my readers say. 'Now for the excuses.'

First came the Londos-Steele match. This lasted over an hour or, in boxing time, over 20 rounds. As the press unanimously agreed, this was the wrestling match of the century. It was fabulous—no other word described it. Londos fought throughout

Karl Pojello, Prenier Wrestler to the Czar of Russia and trainer in USA of the author. An intellectual, Pojello spoke 6 languages.

as if inspired, eventually winning with a new grip to which Steele objected but which, to my mind, was perfectly fair.

My opponent, Babe Caddock, was lighter than I was and should have offered me no difficulty after Zelezniak, Berger and Tragos. He was of course a leading champion or he would not have been given the match. Karl reckoned he was of much the same ability as Tragos. I did not think so.

I entered the ring with a feeling of oppression and claustrophobia. The fantastic number of people all round the ring and stretching far above it, seemingly right up to the sky, was positively frightening. All the earlier contestants were saying this as they returned to the dressing room.

Babe of course felt the same way. Except for Londos and Steele we all seemed paralysed and unable to move, as in a dream where you are being chased and your legs seem leaden. Londos and Steele apparently were accustomed to this feeling, but the rest of us were not and many of the upsets at the Yankee Stadium that night were due to this terrible feeling of oppression.

My memory, perhaps just as well, is dim and obscure. I remember shaking hands and getting that leaden feeling all over. Caddock, too, felt it and was very slow. He defended all the time, leaving me to make the attacks. Try as I would he countered or blocked every hold. I recollect the referee telling him to put some action into it and stop stalling. At one time he lay flat at full length. The crowd did not like it. Nor did I. Redoubling my effort (it was a one-fall match with no rounds, and some time had gone by), I still could not get a hold. It is very difficult to beat an opponent who lies flat in wrestling or one who, in boxing, backpedals and covers up.

My mistake in this match was to do exactly what Babe wanted me to do—lose my temper. To lose control of one's temper in wrestling, or boxing, is to invite defeat. I remember someone shouting, 'What's goin' on, Babe? Don't go to sleep.' In desperation I hauled him to his feet and buttocked him. The buttock—a full one—put him flat on his back but he turned very fast. We rolled right over. My shoulders touched momentarily, but not simultaneously. The referee immediately gave the match to Caddock on a rolling fall.

At the time I was greatly incensed, as my contract called for a pin fall (i.e. a fall where both shoulders are simultaneously pinned to the mat while the referee counts three) or one submission fall. If I was down so was Caddock, as he rolled over first and both his shoulders touched before mine did.

The crowd took some time to quieten down. I went to Karl but got cold comfort. He quietly said: 'Atol, you make lots of mistakes. You son of a gun never listen. They fix you good. Babe make you look bad. He best staller in States—make anyone look bad. What you care anyway You make big success. Seventeen times you win over champions. Now you go home.'

'I am going to get a return with Caddock,' I said.

'That you are not, my friend,' said Stanislaus Zbyszko who had just come in. 'Wladek and I give you plenty money. You go back to England. Get wrestling organised. Irslinger writes me all go phut since you left. You now great drawing card. Listen to us.' Wladek Zbyszko said, 'That's right, Cap—we'll all help you.'

We went to the Waldorf Astoria and then on to the Paradise Club.

Far into the night we talked of all we would do. How once and for all we would put wrestling in Britain back on the map alongside the glove game which had sent hundreds of fighters insane and thousands of others punch drunk.

It was arranged that I would help to open up Great Britain. Wladek would do the same in Spain, and Carol Nowina (nephew to Wladek) in South America. Paoli would open at the Palais des Sports in Paris, and Pojello in the South of France, with Shikat opening up Germany and Gerstmans Belgium.

While there were many good heavyweights in other European countries, very few existed in Britain. The British leaders were very good in an amateurish way. But compared with Pojello and the American champions they lacked experience and were not outstanding. In the new Catch-as-Catch-Can style Archie McDonald, Frank Angel, Bull Coleman, Bulldog Bill Garnon, Barney O'Brien, Bert Assirati and Len Franklin were the best British heavies at that time. Of the European (or old) Catch-as-Catch-Can, William Templeton was the best, with Douglas Clark and Johanfesson in support.

In Cumberland and Westmorland style we believed Jack Robinson to be unbeatable at his weight. But he was not a full heavyweight. It was clear we should have to find new talent and develop it in Britain. Zbyszko said the way to do this was to run open tournaments and issue challenges to everyone, especially the boxers. Then offer high financial rewards to winners and little or nothing to losers.

'We don't expect you to use your own money,' said Stanislaus Zbyszko. 'We give you all you need.'

'I come over right away,' said Pojello, looking benign. 'I give big prescription all Europe's champions. We make big success. I make you million dollars. I ask Big Bill Bartush, weight 270, come too. He Lithuanian American from Chicago. Bill great wrestler. I train him good. Many other American boys come too.'

I stayed quite some time in the States, travelling with Wladek in his chauffeur-driven, silver-studded Cadillac. We went to Atlantic City, where Wladek pointed out the magnificent houses fronting the sea and then the terrible shanty town at the back of them.

He introduced me to many famous Russians, one of whom I questioned about Rasputin, and he told me: 'Rasputin was a hypnotist. A self-hypnotist. We Russians resented the hold he had over the Czarina through the illness of her young son. We decided to remove him. When he came into the Palace I went up to him and shot him six times in the stomach with my revolver. I took two other revolvers from friends and shot him again and again, pumping bullets into him. He stood smiling at me. I then shot him in the head and he fell down dead.'

'Was he supernatural?'

'Yes.'

Wladek stood 6 ft 4 in, weighed 198 stone, and was educated at Cracow University in Poland. He was a millionaire and spoke twelve languages fluently. He was constantly in the news.

One widely reported story about Zbyszko related to his brush with two taxi drivers, after which he was arrested for assault. In court he said:

'I was walking down the street late that night and these two boys were fighting. I went over and said, "Unless you guys are getting paid why fight!" They were rude to me so I felt they needed a lesson. I took them by their necks and banged their heads together. They fell down, both knocked out. Then a cop arrested me.' Case dismissed!

Before I left America the Zbyszkos took me to meet Jack Dempsey, whom they claimed to have 'discovered'. They considered Jack the greatest attacking heavyweight fighter and Jack Johnson the greatest defensive fighter.

Jack looked in great shape. He said, 'When I started out I worked twenty hours a day. I was so doggone tired I envied the horses. Fighters don't have to work that hard any more.

So ended my stay in America. I made a lot of friends and a lot of money. And I learned that to wrestle or box as a real heavyweight champion you have to go over to the States. Taking on Americans in their own country involves a risk, but for me it paid off.

My view is that it takes a certain amount of guts and courage for an Englishman to go over and fight all comers in the States. Had I known what I was in for I too might have had second thoughts. One thing is certain: had it not been for Pojello's tuition I would have followed the inglorious end of all the other English heavyweights (bar Tommy Farr) who, since Fitzsimmons, have challenged Americans on their own ground. But at least these fellows had the guts to try.

So I left on the Europa. This great ship (then holder of the Blue Riband) was stabilised by four gyroscopes of four tons each to stop her rolling. We met a great storm which forced us to slow down.

The majesty and size of those mountainous seas in a North Atlantic storm quickly brought me back quickly to a sense of proportion. Compared with the great forces of nature the strongest men are only as ants.

With this sobering thought I arrived at Southampton and went back to my home in Hampstead Garden Surburb.

9. I Become European Heavyweight Champion

Soon after my return I went to see Fred Davies, who was still President of the British Wrestling Association. The Association had been issuing books containing the new rules to every wrestler. All those wishing to compete (all tournaments were strictly competitive with no one barred) had only to fill in a form.

The British Wrestling Association then issued each applicant with a licence. This enabled a wrestler to enter any tournament without having to pay anything. No one, who applied, was ever refused a licence. Davies had not only been lightweight champion of the world but he had trained the British Olympic team. No one could have been better suited to this position. He issued me with my licence. 'Well, young man,' said Fred, 'if anyone had told me that you or any British heavyweight could win seventeen contests off the reel against the Yanks in their own country I never would have believed them. How about showing me what you can do.'

I showed him in no uncertain manner: two straight falls in two minutes.

'Yes, he said, 'you're a very different proposition to when you were an amateur. You used to rely on strength in those days. Who has been training you!'

I told him all about Karl Pojello and showed him my press cutting book and my Canadian and American licences.

'I want to go for the European Heavyweight Championship.'

You will have to beat the international champions first. I take it you know that?'

Yes. Can you contact the European Federation! You know all champions.'

Yes I do,' he replied.

Fred told me that wrestling had slackened off during my absence the United States. I told him about the Zbyszko offer. How I was looking for an office, I said, and a secretary who would write to the various halls and stadiums to find out whether they would stage open tournaments.

The Old London Sports Club, originally built by my old friend, millionaire Tommy Gordon, and leased to Harold Lane, had now packed up. I went to see Harold, who told me a new venture was to be started in Kings Street, near Baker Street. This was again to be called 'The London Sports Club'.

'I am certainly going to present wrestling,' Harold told me, 'And boxing too. I have engaged Ron Gregory as matchmaker, and I want you against O'Brien top of the bill. If you agree, this match will be for the British heavyweight championship.'

Terms were fixed and the contract signed. If I won, the contract gave him the option to match me in a European heavyweight championship eliminator versus Marcel Douvinet. The British National Wrestling Association had agreed.

Having made these arrangements I took premises in Archer Street, London WI. These consisted of a gymnasium and offices. In response to an advertisement, Miss Nickols, trained in advertising copy and lay-out, applied for the job of running the office. She was a very capable SecretaIy-Manager. I gave her a free hand in choosing the staff she needed. Her duties were to write to the main halls, and she would allow any wrestlers who wished to train to use the gymnasium without charge.

The first December Tournament received a good entry. Lane's Club was sold out, some two thousand five hundred people being present.

I was intrigued with the wrestling of Bob Gregory: a very good-looking English middleweight, trained in France. The boy looked like Rudolf Valentino and was a sensation. Extremely fast, he showed himself to be a stylish and polished matman. He won his fight with two straight falls.

The Irish heavyweight champion, Barney O'Brien, was also a good-looking, well-built fighter. He stood six feet two inches and weighed fourteen and a halfstone. But I was in top form and knocked him out in seven seconds. Many who were still in the bar missed the fight altogether.

Harold Lane came down to the dressing room.

'You might have given them some sort of a show for their money, Atholl.'

I replied, 'I fight to win, not to give shows.'

'That's all very well,' Harold observed, 'but seven seconds is ridiculous. I turned my head to speak to my neighbour. The next thing I knew was O'Brien crashing down. I never even saw you hit him.'

He was really annoyed. Accustomed to boxing matches, where gentlemanly heavyweights dance round each other, dazzling audiences with scintillating exhibitions of the noble art, Harold evidently was unaccustomed to such inconsiderate behaviour.

'We shall be empty for Douvinet,' he said, sadly, as he lit a Corona Corona.

But Lane's Club was not empty. The Douvinee Oakeley fight took place, and Lane's was sold out a week beforehand. The hall was packed to suffocation!

Fred Davis of the International Federation had been appointed middle man. The match, a world and European championship eliminator, was limited to a maximum of three hours. Bob Gregory had arranged a strong supporting bill, which included King Curtis v. George Boganski, and Norman the Butcher 'The Masked Marvel'. Gregory wrote this caption for 'The Masked Marvel':

'Old Etonian and prominent member of London society. Trained in Tokyo, and challenging everyone everywhere. 15 stone. 6 ft 2 in.'

Norman the Butcher's caption read:

'Here to show the Society Pekinese opposite what a real fighting British heavyweight is like, since he apparently imagines that wrestling heavies are the world-wide joke their boxing confrere are. 15 stone. 6 ft 2 in.

I do not have to tell you who wrote that one!

The semi-final to the main bout featured perhaps the most incredible heavyweight in the world. This was Jim Wango, Champion of all Africa, and internationally known as 'The Black Devil'. Blacker than coal, Jim had been giving exhibitions at the Folies Bergere. He ended each performance by jumping fifteen feet from a balcony onto the stage, landing in the splits.

Wango was on against Jack Ansell, 16 stone, 'The Wandsworth Whale' and brother of Norman the Butcher.

This fight was a sensation. Wango somersaulted over the ropes into a splits and stretched out the blackest of black arms to Fred. The palms of his hands were red. His hair stood up like Struelpeter's. He had a trick of striking his cupped hands against his biceps. This made a noise like a pistol shot, as the trapped air could not escape. In addition to this he had a treble (if there is such a thing) bass voice. Each word was roared out at the audience like a thunderclap.

'The Black Devil' was all that we had heard he was. The match lasted some nine or ten minutes, during which Wango spent most of the time up on Jack's shoulders, or whirling round like the

'Apollo' in orbit. Ansell looked like Sinbad the Sailor in the clutches of the Old Man of the Sea. He just couldn't get rid of Wango no matter what he did.

The match was an absolute riot. With Jim's grimaces, ultra-loud voice and ape-like antics, everyone was convulsed. Harold bit his cigar in two.

But I thought: 'This man is not only a terrific showman but he is also a formidable heavyweight—perhaps the most formidable of all.'

The Norman the Butcher fight was one bloody battle. Norman, terribly rough, and constantly warned by Davis for bare fist punching, was outwrestled by the Etonian.

The three judges and arbitrator upheld Davis when he gave a pin fall to the Marvel after thirty-seven minutes in this one-fall match. So the Marvel's pledge to unmask if defeated was not taken up. No one but Gregory, myself, and his cousin had any idea as to who he was. But in his dressing room a stream of blood poured out of his head mask when he removed it.

I say 'without fear of contradiction (as Patsy Hagate used to say at the Club) that at this time Norman the Butcher was the hardest hitting and by far the most ferocious heavyweight in this country.

In the main match, which lasted two hours, I found Douvinet a highly experienced and scientific matman. He was not however in very good shape. Being myself in top form I outstayed him. He became tired and I forced a submission. In a later match Marcel came into the ring at Blackfriars in perfect condition. On that occasion it took me three hours and twenty five minutes before he gave in. At the start of the nineteenth (ten minute) round, the manager of the ring, Victor Berliner, came to my corner and said, 'For heaven's sake, Atholl, finish him off. I want to go home.'

I said, 'If I could I would.'

Soon after, Douvinet became so tired that all resistance vanished and he 'tapped' to a stepover toe hold.

Marcel Douvinet was an exceedingly courteous and polite Frenchman. He was over forty-five years of age and had been wrestling professionally for over thirty years. As George Hackenschmidt says in his book, The Way to Live, these highly experienced wrestlers know all the tricks of the trade and are very hard to beat.

Marcel Douvinet, Champion of Paris, who fought the author for more than three hours at the Ring, Blackfriars, in the longest fight ever recorded in Britain.

After defeating the champion of Paris I then defeated Francois Berthod, the 18 stone heavyweight champion of France. Then the champions of Hungary, Holland, Belgium, Spain, Portugal and other European countries.

In the final I beat the German champion, and champion of Europe, Heinrich Froehner, and so became the new European heavyweight champion.

Some years later Froehner regained the title only to lose it again, almost immediately, to Karl Pojello. Karl was representing the country of his birth, Lithuania.

Wrestling was now drawing packed houses all over Europe. In Monte Carlo I defeated the new Hungarian champion, Karolyi.

In France I won over Lacine, the 9 ft 3 in circus giant who was challenging all comers at weightlifting. I offered to wrestle him but he only laughed. However Pojello and I got hold of his manager and offered him the French equivalent of fifty pounds if I failed to beat his giant. This he accepted. The giant wore a heavy leather belt such as continental weightlifters and Turkish wrestlers wear.

I got one foot up onto his belt, climbed up and hooked the other round his neck, finally locking my two legs together, and, with a body twist, I pulled him over by his neck. He fell heavily, crashing onto the grass. He seemed shaken and declined to go on. The crowd of about two hundred clapped but said nothing.

'Why you no go for legs!' said Karl.

I had many matches in France and won all of them. In England, international wrestlers were arriving in swarms. Pojello had brought over Big Bill Bartush, a 19 stone giant from Chicago. Karl looked after him like a baby. They shared a room in Paris near the Gare du Nord. One day Bill said, 'How about a coffee?'

Karl, writing, looked up and said, 'Ver you fellows go!'

'Just down to Montmartre,' answered Bill.

Bill and I went off and did not return till a couple of hours later. A very indignant and angry Pojello met us:

'Ver you go, Bill Bartush! I know. You no tell me. You go mit girls. You drink too I guess. How you expect vin tomorrow when you do such bad things!'

A few days later, when training, Bartush put a head scissors on me. I came out of it with a thick ear—a beauty. Bill said, 'Each time you look in mirror you think of Bill Bartush, Chicago champ.' Forty years later I am still thinking of Bill Bartush, Chicago champ.

The Hon David Tennant asked Bob Gregory and me if we would wrestle an exhibition at his Gargoyle Club—a highly fashionable rendezvous for London society.

He wanted Bob to wrestle Micky Flack, known as 'The White Owl'. Micky was later drowned crossing the Channel in a canoe, (For the superstitious, the white owl is a sign of death.) He wanted me to wrestle—who else!—Norman the Butcher!

The idea of anyone expecting Norman the Butcher to wrestle an exhibition struck both Bob and me as hilarious.

David Tennant warned us that we must go nowhere near Margot, Lady Oxford (widow of Herbert Asquith the former Prime Minister), who was sitting in the second row at the far end of the long room.

As I have told you Norman, who had started out as an inoffensive six footer, had turned into the biggest crowd puller of all. He had also become the hardest hitting bare-knuckle fighter since Tom Cribb.

So, although he did not use foul holds, he did use his fists and had a supreme contempt for glove-fighters, wrestlers and anyone whom the public regarded as a hero. In particular for me.

Before the fight David Tennant again told the Butcher, first, that he was to put on a gentlemanly exhibition of the new American Catch-as-Catch-Can, and, secondly, that he was not to go near Lady Oxford. He even showed Norman her place in the second row at the far end of the ballroom. I watched the Butcher as he noted her chair. After the preliminary bout, Bob Gregory v. The White Owl (which was a beautiful exhibition), I went in followed by the Butcher. Norman looked like Mephistopheles in his yellow dressing gown with its skull and crossbones. With beetling black eyebrows and his great black, hair-covered chest he was something none of these aristocrats had ever seen before. I watched Lady Oxford's look of utter astonishment as she first looked at me and then at Norman the Butcher. Behind her I saw Sir Oswald Mosley also looking surprised, as well he might.

Fred Davis, the referee, gave us a quick briefing: there were to be no falls, just a scientific clean exhibition of the new wrestling. 'And no nonsense,' he said to Norman.

Now Davis, immaculate in his dinner jacket, stood in the middle of the floor. David Tennant announced the exhibitions.

'Right, fall to,' says Fred.

The next instant I felt a stunning blow on my right eye. Then I was high above the Butcher's head, and found myself flying through the air straight at Lady Oxford. I fell on the chair in front, but six stalwart young men (presumably there to Protect her) prevented my rolling over.

As Norman should have known, this was not a nice thing to do at all. It could get us a bad name, especially after the elegant and highly scientific exhibition by Bob and The White Owl.

Fred was furious and took Norman on one side. What he said I can't imagine. However, the Butcher, like all of us, admired Fred Davis, and after this unfortunate start an 'exhibition' followed and was well received in polite silence. A full page picture appeared next day in the Daily Mirror. We were progressing!

The next important event in the wrestling world was the advent of Jack Baltus, born on Exmoor. Jack stood over 7 ft in his socks and weighed 26 st 7 Ibs. I took one look at him and promptly named him 'Carver Doone'.

Shortly afterwards a giant Scotsman arrived from Fraserburgh, near Aberdeen. This was no less a person than the mammoth John Bell, who stood 6 ft 1 in, tipped the scale at 30 stone and was heavyweight champion of Scotland. His discoverer was my old wrestling friend from the Ashdown, Angus McShayne. He was followed by George Clark, the Highland Games Champion and record holder, who came from Dundee. George was 6 ft 3 in, a finely built man of great strength, weighing around 17 stone or a little less.

Karl meantime had discovered Dave Armstrong, a fine 6 ft heavyweight from Choppington, near Newcastle-on-Tyne, Dave challenged me at Lane's Club and after tuition by Karl took me to sixty-two minutes before he submitted, after one of the finest matches (so Lane said) seen at the club.

At this time I opened a training camp at Cublington. Dave Armstrong, Stanley Powton, Carver Doone, John Bell and myself, put ourselves under the Lancashire champion and British lightweight champion Richard Wills. One day in walked Jumbo Giles, who had been my company cook in the Oxfordshire and Buckinghamshire Light Infantry.

'Come to join the wrestlers, sir,' said Jumbo, who weighed thirty two stone. 'Challenge everyone, sir. Even you, sir, soon as I get fit,

John Bell and Carver listened in amazement to this speech. John went round telling everyone: 'Heard the latest news, sir! Jumbo Giles has joined the wrestlers, sir. Talk of Oxford, sir. Challenging everyone, sir. Whatever shall we do, sir!'

Dick and I strapped three mattresses round Jumbo and another three round John. We made them run twice round the field three times a day. After the first circuit Jumbo, sweat running down his face like Niagara Falls, stopped where I was standing and called out: 'I can run no more, sir. If you want more running, sir, you must run yourself, sir. John Bell, just behind, called out, That goes for me too, sir. We got Jumbo down four stone in four weeks and John Bell two stone.

One day I drove Dave and John ten miles out in my car telling them we were going for road work. I then told them to get out, and run home. They arrived back three hours later. Long afterwards I heard Dave telling the story:

'We, went into a pub. Had a drink and rang up for a taxi. Ran the last hundred yards and saw Atholl in a deck chair. "Well done, chaps," he said. 'Of course he never knew.'

After the month's training had ended Jumbo followed me around issuing challenges. A promoter wanted the match, but I explained Jumbo had been in my platoon and I couldn't possibly fight him. However he pointed out Jumbo was an immense man and if I kept refusing his challenge people might think I was afraid of him. Any wrestling tuition at the camp had been under Dick Wills, not me. I had never wrestled Giles but knew from what the others said that he was very strong, although short-winded.

The match duly took place. After six minutes I got behind Jumbo and brought him down with the same hold I used on Casey Berger. He lay like a huge whale marooned on the beach, so I face-locked him. With a great shout, which must have been heard in the street, Jumbo called out, ' I'm done, sir.

The howl of laughter which greeted this I never heard before or since. John Bell, who was on the same bill, went around for days saying: 'Talk of Oxford, sir, nearly flopped the captain, sir.'

'The Masked Marvel' was never beaten but gave up wrestling here as he was due, I believe, to return to Japan. He told me an incident which took place at the time of all the press publicity before his first fight, when he was sitting in a famous West End Services Club. 'Damned vulgar blowing Eton all over the papers, don't you think!' asked a colonel.

'Yes', replied the Marvel, 'I don't agree with it either.

Only three of us ever knew who he was. But, long afterwards, his niece, Fiona, came on my yacht to learn advanced navigation.

'I hear you were a wrestling champion,' she said. 'My uncle was also a champion. He was trained in Japan. He was very good, I believe.'

'Yes, he certainly was,' I answered.

10. A Brush with the Underworld

Norman the Butcher, Aussie the Butcher, 'Hard-boiled' Herbie Rosenberg, Jack Pye, 'Gentleman Jim' and 'Black Butcher' Johnson were regarded as 'villains' by the people who came to watch, but they were all in their own way big crowd pullers. Norman, the roughest man in Europe, was the arch-villain. Jack Pye, a former miner from Doncaster, a heavyweight of outstanding: ability, had been discovered by the ex-amateur British lightweight champion, Harold Angus. Jack stopped almost at nothing. Tough as nails, he was chosen to represent Britain in the great tournament at the Victoria Palace. Aided by Jack Payne's band the first weeks of this tournament broke every attendance record for the Palace. Wrestling for the 'foreigners' were Jim Wango (The Black Devil), Marcel Douvinet, Francois Berthod and Henri Letailleur. For the home team—myself, Norman the Butcher, Len Franklin and Jack Pye.

On the first night General Critchley, of the GRA, brought Primo Carnera, and they sat in the stage box. Knowing Primo as a wrestler (he was at this time world heavyweight boxing champion) I waited for the curtain. As soon as it was raised I stepped forward, in full wrestling kit, and challenged Carnera there and then to come down and wrestle me!

Primo was obviously taken aback and at once there was bedlam. No one, least of all the general, had expected this denouement. Slowly the giant Italian stood up and, in his great bass voice, got as far as 'I am not prepared ...' when I called out: 'We have wrestling kit here for you, Primo. Come on down.' The general, the sporting journalists and the management were absolutely livid at this showing up of the World Heavyweight Boxing Champion. Primo was in a cleft stick, as I intended he should be.

Readers should appreciate that he was essentially a Graeco Roman wrestler. If he accepted the challenge he knew I could, and would, beat him in the American style of which he then had no knowledge. If he refused it showed the public the strength of the modern world heavyweight boxing championship in comparison with the world heavyweight wrestling championship.

After the show I had a flaming row with three boxing journalists, and the next day I had another with the general. He told me that had he known I intended to use the occasion to 'discredit boxing' he would not have come.

The Victoria Palace Tournament was 'American'; i.e. one where everyone wrestled everyone else. It went on the whole week. Booked through an agent, its success depended entirely on Jim Wango The management had refused to accept it for more than one week, and everyone told them it would not draw peanuts.

In vain I pointed out that the foreigners needed Ministry per mission for a further appearance and that, unless application was made at once for a second week, Wango and his team could only compete during the first week. Without Wango I emphasised it would not be full every night.

During the first week 'House Full' notices went up for each evening and for the matinees. Although I survived undefeated, and defeated Jim Wango in the final, the team victory went to the foreigners. It was an outstanding success both from the point of view of the gate receipts and the spectacle. On the Saturday night, the manager implored me to try to get the foreign team to stay over and re-wrestle the tournament during the following week. But the Ministry said 'no so the Palace threw away a golden opportunity. Later, however, similar tournaments were held in five provincial theatres. Jack Pye, after contests every night, seemed to thrive on continuous fighting for five weeks. But for me the week at the Victoria Palace was enough. I was stiff and sore all over. 'Anyone can see you never worked in the pits,' said Jack.

Norman the Butcher was to feature in an episode which nearly got us into trouble. The Graf Zeppelin, Germany's monster airship nearly as long as the Queen Elizabeth, was due to arrive at what is now Heathrow. The authorities anticipated some four million people would want to see the airship. Before the Zeppelin arrived they asked us to stage four wrestling fights. Norman the Butcher v. Henri Letailleur of France was to be the main bout. Then I heard they proposed using Daily Mail screens to enclose a few thousand chairs around the ring.

I said, 'Do you mean to say you only expect a few thousand out of four million to watch the wrestling! You must be mad.'

'How many do you think will want to watch wrestling ~' they asked.

'Out of four million—half. Say two million. You will have to erect a fence.)

'You must be joking, was the reply.

Norman arrived driving an open Bentley 3 litre and accompanied by a beautiful girl wearing a fur coat and a picture hat (fashionable at the time). He headed straight down the main runway reserved for the airship.

Angry officials tried to intercept him but scattered right and left when he drove at them. Having parked the Bentley in the VIP enclosure, Norman left his girl and went over to the enclosure where a light aircraft was engaged in taking people up for twenty-minute fights. Having had his offer (two seats for the wrestling in exchange for a seat in the aircraft) accepted, Norman went up.

On coming down the pilot said: 'This man is crackers. He told me, "This is too tame. Let's loop.

In vain the pilot had argued that his plane could not loop the loop.

Finally he brought Norman down and I-reported him.

Meantime, the authorities had given me permission to address the public over the loudspeakers. No one interrupted me, so I spent over an hour extolling the fighting qualities of Norman the Butcher.

My publicity was quite effective. The crowd went over to the wrestling enclosure en masse. They flattened the Daily Mail screens, occupied every chair and every foot of grass, in front, beside and behind the chairs, and never paid a halfpenny.

A man said to me:

'Now you know what's wrong with British business.'

'What!' I asked.

'Everything, he said.

The end came when Norman the Butcher knocked Henri Letailleur out and into the audience. An angry Frenchman called him a 'cochon', so Norman vaulted over the ropes and knocked him out too.

Weeks later, Irslinger invited me to lunch with Eckener, the Zeppelin commander, at the Savoy. Eckener told me that he had made over a hundred and sixty uneventful trips to South America. Passengers were housed as if in a hotel with baths, writing rooms and private cabins. They could walk through the envelope from stem to stern. If a storm approached Eckener took the ship above it, or, if he was unable to avoid it, he hove her to on the port tack. He was bitter over the refusal of the Americans to supply him with helium, which meant it had to be filled with hydrogen. Eckener was not in command when, later, the highly inflammable hydrogen was ignited by static electricity as the Hindenberg was being moored to her pylon in New Jersey. A spark turned the dirigible into a flaming hell from which only one man escaped.

If the national press in England wrote up only the most sensational events in wrestling, all the provincial press rose magnificently to the occasion. Before my matches at Nottingham, Bristol and other cities, marvellous write-ups appeared and afterwards there were long reports accurately describing the fights and even the holds used, all written by provincial pressmen who understood wrestling. Only when the London national press realised that they were on the losing end of their fight to stop wrestling from ousting boxing did they begin to relent.

One day the Evening Standard sent a reporter to 'try a fall' with me.

Later a long article was printed together with a picture.

'Why have you not done this before!' I asked.

'You had better ask the boys at the top,' he replied. 'Surely you know there is a ban by the national press on wrestling?'

This article considerably increased London's interest in the new sport. The 'Ring' and 'Lanes' had 'Full House' notices every night. At Brixham Stadium 14,000 people came to see me beat Zaranoff, and over 13,000 came to see me beat 'The Black Eagle', a very strong coloured heavyweight.

It was at a third match that London gangsters came into my dressing room at Brixton.

'We have bets on —,' they said. 'Tonight you will lose.'

Threats and requests to lose matches had always amused me. Whatever could be said of other professional sports, no leading fighter in those days ever took a dive in any wrestling match or mixed 'wrestler v. boxer' fight.

I won. But as I was about to take a shower four men, one a British heavyweight, pushed open the dressing-room door. When one has nothing on four men with open cut-throat razors are not a pleasant sight.

'This is where you finish up, Oakeley,' said the leader, a strong and heavily built British wrestler.

But he had bargained without Richard Wills of Newbiggin. Wills was then the Light-heavyweight champion of Great Britain. The finest wrestler ever produced by England, Dick Wills had for years been a 'match wrestler' in Lancashire. There is no record of his ever having been defeated by anyone at his own weight. For years and years he had fought, for side-stakes, and these matches took place every Saturday afternoon against opponents brought by their backers from all over the country. 3000 or more Paid 9d each to watch, while the side-stakes often reached £1000 and the winning wrestler received a percentage. All fights were in the Lancashire Catch-as-Catch-Can style. Wills, a coal miner, was without fear.

To say a man is 'without fear' is a bold assertion. In a long life I have met only five. Captain Harry Daniels, v.c., Field-Marshal Alexander, my sergeant at Sandhurst, Jack Sherry and Dick Wills.

Whereas virtually all men feel fear, the brave are able to conquer it. But these men never felt fear at all. I saw Daniels, who could not swim, dive off the top board at the Army Headquarters' pool in Aldershot. Diving too steeply he went over backwards, ripping his back on the bottom of the bath. With blood pouring from the cuts, he was pulled out by the C.S.M.I. Whereupon he did twelve more dives, each time being hauled out.

I asked him if he had conquered fear.

'No,' he said. 'I do not know what it feels like to be afraid so there is nothing to conquer.'

'How did you get the V.C.!'

'The Brigadier happened to be looking.

When, therefore, Dick Wills interposed himself between the four and me, it came as a surprise to the four gangsters. 'Get out of the way, Dick,' said the wrestler. But Dick never moved a muscle. I watched his face. It was expressionless.

Meantime the giant Carver Doone had gone out for the police.

Every other British wrestler in the dressing room had vanished. For a full minute no one spoke.

Dick said, 'You do Atholl, you have to do me.' I saw the leader, an arrogant bully, then hesitate. Slowly the four closed their razors, turned round, and walked out.

When the police arrived we were asked for the names of the men. 'They've gone,' I replied. 'No damage done. Call it a day.'

When I thanked Dick and Carver, the former said, 'When gangsters are four against someone who is unarmed they become arrogant. But if two stand up and don't try to run, it upsets them.'

"Were you scared!'

'X would not attack me like that. They all expected to get you alone with your clothes off.'

The fact that we did not give names to the police was duly appreciated by the underworld. I was never bothered again. Long after, the father of one of them apologised to me on his deathbed and thanked me for not divulging the name of his son, who had learned his lesson. The doctrine of 'an eye for an eye' breeds only bitterness. Whereas unexpected generosity and mercy—shown once and once only-generally takes the intelligent criminal by surprise. But as the Chinese say: 'He who is bitten once by a dog suffers bad luck. He who is bitten a second time is a fool and deserves it.'

I bore no malice against this wrestler. Several years later I matched him on one of my biggest promotions. We never referred to the razor incident, but I never forgot my debt to the little coalminer whose absence of fear that day saved me. It was a very near shave!

11. British Wrestling Hits the Big-time

While wrestling attendances were booming, those for boxing were falling off everywhere except in London.

Our offices were now under the management of Mrs. Covell, with Freda Jackson as secretary and Paula Phillips in charge of publicity. Assisted by a well-trained staff, Mrs. Covell dealt with promoters from all over Great Britain, and she was responsible for organising the preliminary bouts. The top billings requested by promoters had to be referred to the Association, and in this way repetition was, as far as possible, avoided. In the main bouts the winner took a percentage of the receipts, while the loser took much less. Only star top-liners were allowed managers, so lesser lights kept all the money made in the preliminaries.

Whereas boxers, by virtue of the knocking about they received, and the resultant facial cuts and injuries, could only box at fairly long intervals, wrestlers, enjoying their body-building sport, thought nothing of wrestling five preliminaries a week. The champions, having more to gain if they won and more to lose if they lost, fought between one and three matches a week, and sometimes less than this.

With the exception of people like Bernard Gray, P. J. Moss, Peter Wilson and J. W. Drawbell, publicity was hard to get. The whole of the national press almost seemed under orders to smash wrestling. On every possible occasion, whenever they wrote about it at all, they seemed to lampoon it with sarcastic cracks and unfair innuendoes.

My personal publicity, however, ably handled by Christopher Mann, left nothing to be desired. No matter what vested interests were involved, or what 'directives' may have been issued by Proprietors of the national press, the British provincial newspapers continued to headline my every appearance in their cities and always carried column upon column about the fights.

Undoubtedly it was the publicity given with the utmost fairness by all the provincial papers that broke the national press's ban, smashed boxing in the provinces and put wrestling back on the map in Britain.

Pojello and myself issued weekly challenges to every boxer in the world and £500 to anyone, bare fists, gloved fists or otherwise, who could knock us out. As a result, the nationals had little alternative but to pay some attention to the sport.

Then one morning Mrs. Covell did not arrive at the office. At eleven o'clock Scotland Yard detectives arrived to tell us she had been murdered. We had lost a very good friend and a first-class Organiser. Freda took over while I looked around for someone to replace her.

But this was well-nigh an impossibility. Mrs. Covell was highly experienced and knew everything there was to know about the preliminaries. She was also person grata with the promoters. I was at my wits' end when Vivian Van Damm came to see me one day, accompanied by his American manager, Teddy Elbin.

'I have a choice,' he said, 'of opening the Windmill Cinema as a burlesque house or going into wrestling. Cut me in and I go into your sport. But on one condition.'

'What condition!' I asked.

'That you agree to Teddy organising.'

Elbin had seen the money that the new style was making in the States. He also believed that, in consequence of my American success, and my 'social standing (as he called it), I could be built it to a great international drawing card'.

I liked Teddy and I liked Van Damm. Both were astute business men who looked further than their noses. They knew what the public wanted, and that was not boxing, which, as they rightly said, appealed to the women less than wrestling.

Having agreed on terms Elbin asked me if I would fight a West Indian heavyweight as top of the bill at a charity tournament he intended to promote at Maidenhead.

His American-style publicity packed the open-air ground. After I had defeated the beautifully muscled, ebony Phil Siki, in a clean and fast fight, Teddy sent a note to the dressing room asking me to meet him at the bar of the club.

I found him there in the company of quite the most glamourous woman, outside the Ziegfeld Follies, that I had ever seen. Elbin, who did nothing by halves, was obviously well aware of the sensation his Venus must be making. She was dressed in palest blue with a matching picture hat; the 'Ensemble Parisienne'.

I remember thinking: 'What a wonderful-looking couple these two are. Teddy Elbin, with his immaculate Savile Row suit, and this gorgeous female.'

'My secretary,' said Elbin.

'How do you do!' asked Venus. 'You were marvellous. How did you get that physique!'

'Hard exercise,' chuckled Elbin. 'Now if you will come with me, Mr. Oakeley, we have a contract for you to sign.' He led the way up to the office, where I read the contract and, objecting to one of the clauses, dictated a revision. His secretary took it down in shorthand.

Then we went back into the club. Elbin asked me to call at Van Damm's London offices the following morning and sign the agreement. I said goodbye and left them.

Half an hour later Teddy left the club by himself. Within the hour he was dead, victim of a hit-and-run accident. As he was crossing the main London road, a car, driven at an estimated speed of over seventy miles an hour, sent him, and Van Damm's wrestling proposition into Eternity. Without Elbin, Vivian felt too inexperienced to go through with the wrestling promotion and 'phoned me, to this effect, the following morning. 'I am going to put on non-stop revue at the Windmill' he told me.

Meantime Teddy's secretary had asked us whether we needed a chief executive. We took the opportunity and, in this position Kathleen Look began her long association with wrestlers, later becoming, beyond all doubt, Europe's most outstanding promoter of this sport.

On the axiom that 'Manchester leads where other's follow' she decided that this great city, in the centre of a community which liked and understood wrestling, afforded her the opportunity to establish world championship wrestling in this country.

Since I had returned from America, Henry Iles, who was said to be the power behind the throne at Belle Vue, Manchester, had resolutely refused to allow wrestling at the King's Hall.

Now we checked up on Iles movements and, having found out that he travelled from London to Manchester each week on a certain day and by a certain train, we arranged for the glamorous Kathleen to travel on the same train.

A day or two later, Kathleen came back with the Belle Vue contract. This was what she told Pojello and myself:

'I arrived suitably attired at Euston. Having duly recognised Mr. Iles from your description, I got into his carriage and sat opposite him. He was reading the newspaper. Some time after the train left he put down his paper and asked whether I minded if he shut the window. I replied I would welcome it. He then asked me if I was going to Manchester. I replied that I was going there on business.

'"You look too glamorous for business," he said. "May I ask what kind of business?"

'The poor gentleman seemed shaken to the soles of his shoes when I told him I was a wrestling promoter. He then told me that he had staged the first of the two All-In wrestling tournaments ever promoted in England.

'I asked him who participated in the main bout. "Oh," he said, "that Atholl Oakeley who is responsible for the whole business. I expect you know him!"

'"Yes," I answered. "He is my technical adviser on wrestling. If you give me the contract for the Belle Vue Promotion I guarantee you will not regret it."

'"On one condition," replied Iles. "That you, and not Atholl Oakeley, are the promoter."'

So began a business relationship which built up Belle Vue, Manchester, into Europe's greatest and best known wrestling stadium. Its fame spread far and wide. The wrestling world was intrigued by a 'lady promoter'. Even Mrs. Henri Irslinger joined in the fun and became a promoter. But none had the beauty, brains or glamour of Kathleen Look.

Bernard Gray of the Daily Mirror once said to her: 'Miss Look, I have to be satisfied, before I write up your tournaments, that they are genuine.' Kathleen at once replied: 'I can easily prove that by doing what your boxing promoters should do. I will advertise clearly7 that no one is barred, and that the winner of the annual championship tournament will be guaranteed a title fight with the world heavyweight champion: in other words, the man who can prove that he is the undisputed champion of the world. We will further offer £5000 to any boxer or wrestler who can defeat this champion.'

'Do you really mean that!' asked Bernard. 'It sounds fantastic. Who is this man!'

'Jack Sherry of Alaska, I replied. The greatest heavyweight fighter, and the strongest since Milo of Croton.'

'But will you get this man to wrestle here?'

'Atholl can get the champions,' says Kathleen. 'They would all come for him.'

Thereafter, Bernard Gray never faltered in his opinion that it would be quite impossible for anyone to fur the result of these tournaments. He gave Kathleen wonderful notices, column after column, and he got colleagues in the north to follow suit.

But my own wrestling career was soon to come to a close. In all I had won over two thousand fights. No British professional had ever beaten me, and only four foreign champions had gained decisions over me.

One of these was Pojello, whom I met at Bradford and was defeated by a fall in some fifty-five minutes. It was a marvellous fight, but it is very hard for the apprentice to beat the master.

Throughout the fight he taunted me, as Jack Johnson had taunted Burns at Reno.

'Vat you do, Atol? You dam lazy. Vy you no beat zis old man? You young fellow. You not fight. You just Palooka. See, you no hold me down. I escape all you try. Now you old man. You get tired. Mr. Pojello never tired. He wrestle all day, all night, all time like cat. Vot good I teach you ven you no beat old man!'

Enraged, I tried everything in (and out of) the book. It was all no good. In the end I got caught in seven successive chain holds, escaped six, and ended up nearly torn in half by Karl's famous Lithuanian Spreadeagle.

Most vicious was my fight with the gigantic lumberjack Carver Doone, at Hull. Carver stood seven feet or more and weighed in at 26 st 4 lbs. He was magnificently built, carried no fat and, like George Hill, was as strong as an ox. He had started off as a camp fighter in Canada, then taken up professional boxing and then, as there was more money in it, turned to wrestling.

no one is barred, and that the winner of the annual championship tournament will be guaranteed a title fight with the world heavyweight champion: in other words, the man who can prove that he is the undisputed champion of the world. We will further offer £5000 to any boxer or wrestler who can defeat this champion.'

'Do you really mean that?' asked Bernard. 'It sounds fantastic. Who is this man!'

'Jack Sherry of Alaska, I replied. The greatest heavyweight fighter, and the strongest since Milo of Croton.'

'But will you get this man to wrestle here?'

'Atholl can get the champions,' says Kathleen. 'They would all come for him.'

Thereafter, Bernard Gray never faltered in his opinion that it would be quite impossible for anyone to fix the result of these tournaments. He gave Kathleen wonderful notices, column after column, and he got colleagues in the north to follow suit.

But my own wrestling career was soon to come to a close. In all I had won over two thousand fights. No British professional had ever beaten me, and only four foreign champions had gained decisions over me.

One of these was Pojello, whom I met at Bradford and was defeated by a fall in some fifty-five minutes. It was a marvellous fight, but it is very hard for the apprentice to beat the master. Throughout the fight he taunted me, as Jack Johnson had taunted Burns at Reno.

'Vat you do, Atol! You dam lazy. Vy you no beat zis old man? You young fellow. You not fight. You just Palooka. See, you no hold me down. I escape all you try. Now you old man. You get tired. Mr. Pojello never tired. He wrestle all day, all night, all time like cat. Vot good I teach you ven you no beat old man!'

Enraged, I tried everything in (and out of) the book. It was all no good. In the end I got caught in seven successive chain holds, escaped six, and ended up nearly torn in half by Karl's famous Lithuanian Spreadeagle.

Most vicious was my fight with the gigantic lumberjack Carver Doone, at Hull. Carver stood seven feet or more and weighed in at 26 st 4 lbs. He was magnificently built, carried no fat and, like George Hill, was as strong as an ox. He had started off as a camp fighter in Canada, then taken up professional boxing and then, as there was more money in it, turned to wrestling.

He had fought three bloody bare-fist prize fights (no other words describe them) with Norman the Butcher at the Ring, Blackfriars. unless one booked seats weeks before it was impossible to get in for the third and last of these Carver-Butcher contests.

I fought Carver to a sixty-minute draw at Hull. For nearly all that time he legitimately pulled down both knuckles from way above his seven-foot-high head onto the back of my neck. Rabbit punching like this, even though you have a 22 inch neck like me, makes you giddy. Carver's blows were none too accurate and many of these guillotine blows went down my back, so high up above me he towered.

My English manager, Phil Meader, called in the doctor afterwards. They reckoned there was not one square inch of my back, or back of my neck, which was not as black as that of a coloured man.

Carver and I wrestled some three times but never again did I give him a chance to use his 'guillotine-rabbit-punches". Had it not been for the years over which I used to pull out the steel neck exerciser, I feel sure Carver would have broken my neck that night in Hull (I nearly wrote 'Hell'!).

On each subsequent occasion I lost no time in getting behind him and winning with my usual hammer lock and stepover toe hold.

Carver was a well-educated and highly intelligent man. He also had a magnificent tenor voice. Once, when he returned from Manchester in the dickey of my Chrysler, he sang opera for over four hours. When we stopped at an all-night transport cafe and Carver walked in with Dick Wills, everyone got up and rushed out. It took ten minutes before they were sufficiently reassured to return. That same night a lorry, driven by a six-foot coloured man, cut in on us, and we pulled him up. He got out of the cab shouting 'You wanna make something! Get the hell outa there.' One of the funniest sights imaginable was the speed with which he got back in again when Carver got out with all his seven foot looming up in our headlights.

Norman the Butcher had a keen sense of humour. Once King Curtis and he were off to Newcastle. As I walked up the platform I saw King and Norman wearing red wigs and looking like orangoutangs. On the carriage window was a notice: 'lunatics. Keep out.'

After my retirement I was driving Norman in my 100 mph Ford V8 on the old Roman Road near Tamworth. We were bowling along at 90 mph when we saw a Baby Austin ahead. The driver had' his hand out to turn right. (There were no flashing lights in those days.) 'Drive up alongside,' says Norman.

Alongside, down to the same speed as the Austin, Norman leant out, grasped the hand of the driver (a clergyman) in a vice-like grip and said, 'How do you do? How nice to meet you!' The poor man missed his turning and looked quite flabbergasted. I wonder whether he will read this!

Then one evening my end came suddenly and unexpectedly.

Wrestling at Southend against Len Franklin (the English southern champion and my very goon friend from amateur days) I lifted him overhead, slipped, and fell with his full weight on top of me. I fell on my right shoulder, breaking and dislocating it.

Karl wanted me to have the Russian 'Nicolaev' operation (where the head of the humerus is wired on). But no one in England then appeared to have experience of this. They all wanted me to have the acromium process built up, as England's champion high jumper, Howard Baker, did.

I waited about six months and then tackled Van Dutz at Oxford. But my shoulder again slipped out. I whispered, 'Shoulder's gone, Izzy. instantly he released his hold and stood up. The fight was declared null and void through injury. It was the end. I never wrestled again. My career as a fighter was over.

12. Jack Sherry, the Greatest of Them All

My retirement was greeted with dismay by promoters, not only in Britain and Ireland, but throughout all Europe. Naturally, interested in drawing as many people to their tournaments as possible, they found themselves without one whom they regarded as their star attraction. In addition to this nearly all their wrestlers had, at some time or other, been beaten by me.

These were the unpalatable facts which faced the wrestling world this side of the Atlantic at the end of 1935. Obviously something had to be done. Providence again stepped in when I received a cable from Henri in South Africa.

> Have greatest heavyweight world has ever seen. Stop.
> He is killing our Houses. Stop.
> Name Jack Sherry holds World Title. Stop.
> Am sending him to you before he puts me out of business. Henri.

Bulldog Bill Garnon, Heavyweight Champion of Wlaes, whose fight with the author, filmed by Paramount, was undoubtedly one of the bloodiest battles since the days of the prize ring.

Of course everyone in the USA knew of Sherry. As in boxing there were two wrestling 'groups'. Each was bitterly opposed to the other, and each had its own 'world champion'. Competition to find a heavyweight champion who could beat the other was intense. At this time Jack Curley had all the best heavyweights: Stanislaus Zbyszko had been three times world champion and was the former Diamond Belt holder. Wladek Zbyszko had also held the crown. Together with Hans Steinke, whom no one could beat, Curley had Ed Lewis who was also unbeatable.

The opposition had Everett Marshall, a magnificently built man, more handsome than many film stars. He was also a first-class heavyweight who, in some states, was regarded as the world champion. But although Everett was a brilliant champion, well able to hold his own against 99 per cent of the world's heavyweights, the two aces, Lewis and Steinke, as I have said, were both held by Jack Curley. He also had the two formidable Russians Zelezniac and Kwariani.

While I was in the States the Zbyszkos, who were, as I have said, behind wrestling and to a great extent behind boxing as well, fell out with Curley. Having already introduced nearly every foreign wrestler of repute into America, Stanislaus decided that he was now going to search for one of these 'freak' men like Gotch, or Youssouf of Turkey, who used to beat everyone with ease in the old days. I use 'freak' in no derogatory sense here, but rather to indicate what the science fiction writers describe as a superman, i.e. a man of fabulous strength, far above anyone else, whom no one can tackle without being crushed.

These men are seldom showmen. Generally they cannot attract the crowds and are kept in the background by promoters who prefer to put the best of the faster and lighter men as 'world champions'. In a commercial age this is considered good business. No one pays to see wrestlers or boxers crushed in a second!

Stanislaus, to my knowledge, had had scouts out in Mongolia (where one such man was known to exist). They had also combed Egypt, Abyssinia and India. But, although they found many very strong men, none was adjudged to be capable of beating the kingpin of the Curley Promotions, the one and only Ed 'Saangler' Lewis, then universally recognised, with former champion John Pezek, as the greatest wrestler of modern times.

Lewis, with Ted Thye, had introduced the new wrestling to Australia. In doing so he had netted himself a fortune. This, coupled with his American earnings, made Lewis, like Stanislaus Zbyszko a millionaire many times over. It could be said that, after Farmer Burns and Frank Gotch amalgamated the submission holds of jiu-jitsu (now called Judo) with the pinfalls of Catch-as-Catch-Can, Lewis and Zbyszko were the fathers of modern wrestling.

But Lewis was no longer a young man. He had been on more than one occasion champion of the world on merit. With Steinke in abeyance no one else had had any chance of getting by Ed. Stanislaus, realising this all-important fact, redoubled his efforts to find a young superman' who could force Londos out of the championship and then beat the ageing Ed, in this way wresting the championship out of Curley's hands.

The answer came while I was in the States. It became known in Alaska that Zbyszko was looking for a super wrestler. One day he received a letter from a prospector to the effect that, among the gold miners, there was a man of such phenomenal strength that everyone in Alaska was afraid of him. Now Alaskan miners are not exactly long-haired pop singers. They settle disputes with heavy boots and bare fists, in a climate which would kill most weaker men. Anyone who can terrorise such people must indeed be tough.

Zbyszko took some time to trace this superman. All that was known of him was that he had come to Alaska from Yugoslavia, that his name was Ivan Seric, and that his father and mother had been farmers. He was reputed to weigh only seventeen stone and measure six foot, but so terrific was his power that no man could even get his arm free once this Ivan Seric had grasped his wrist. It was said that he could lift the heaviest miner over his head with one hand and with a single movement. Some declared that he had strangled bears with his bare hands; others that he lifted rocks which no other man in all Alaska could move.

When Stanislaus caught up with Seric, he straight away took him into his private gym. Seric just grabbed the 24 stone, 5 ft 5 in Pole, former champion of the world, by each wrist and slowly forced him flat onto his back. Time 39 seconds, Then he did the same to Wladek. The utter amazement of the Zbyszko brothers can well be imagined. They had discovered their superman.

Moreover, Stanislaus soon found out that Seric was not like, say, former wrestler Primo Carnera, who knew little about boxing and only won the championship by the devastating power of his punches. The Alaskan was well versed in wrestling technique. However, Zbyszko also realised that a heavyweight as experienced and clever as Ed 'Strangler' Lewis might, in a 60 minute world title fight, take evading action and prevent Seric from getting to grips.

During my stay in America Zbyszko had constantly emphasised that super-strong men of little action, like Primo or Galna of India, Godfrey and Steinke, inevitably kill houses for boxing and wrestling.

The public simply will not pay to see a giant beating a pygmy. Wrestling: championships, like those in boxing, must be between very active, fast, small heavyweights, if they are to attract the paying public. Seric obviously could not be said to fit into this category.

Wladek accordingly was detailed further to instruct Ivan in the art of the mat. To his surprise he found that the Yugoslav knew far more than either he or Stanley had imagined to be possible.

Before launching Seric professionally they renamed him. He was not Russian but 'Ivan' suggested that he was. In fact he was an American citizen. They decided therefore that he must have an American name which everyone could remember. With thoughts of the incomparable Jack Dempsey, both voted for 'Jack'. As a second name they wanted one every newsboy could remember.

So they settled for 'Sherry'.

Thus Jack Sherry, the greatest heavyweight fighter and wrestler of modern times, came into being.

This then was the man whose challenges to Londos and all the Curley group had been the talk of America. This was the man who was now the overall and undisputed heavyweight champion of the world. This was the man who, it was said, feared neither man nor beast; a man who challenged everyone and barred no one; whom no one had ever pinned, knocked out or forced to submit. A man who if he chose, could beat anyone in the world in seconds; who had pinned the great Pojello twice in two and a half minutes. A man with whom no boxer, and few wrestlers, would enter the ring!

This was the champion that the one and only Henri was wishing on me. The man who had nearly killed wrestling in South Africa and who could no longer fight in USA as no one would enter the ring with him!

The truth, as I later heard, was that the Zbyszkos had been hoist with their own petard. They had brought in a 'Frankenstein who had destroyed not only their enemies but also their own aims.

Honest to a degree, this fantastic Hercules not only refused to lose for any popular so-called champion, but even refused to give a fall!

In fact his idea of the sport was to wrestle two or three minutes and then leisurely to dispose of any opponent put up against him.

So the challenges of this man upset the world of fighters.

When Lewis beat Londos, so becoming the overall champion of the world, he was then put up to stop this Alaskan challenger. one occasion champion of the world on merit. With Steinke in abeyance no one else had had any chance of getting by Ed. Stanislaus, realising this all-important fact, redoubled his efforts to find a young superman' who could force Londos out of the championship and then beat the ageing Ed, in this way wresting the championship out of Curley's hands.

The answer came while I was in the States. It became known in Alaska that Zbyszko was looking for a super wrestler. One day he received a letter from a prospector to the effect that, among the gold miners, there was a man of such phenomenal strength that everyone in Alaska was afraid of him. Now Alaskan miners are not exactly long-haired pop singers. They settle disputes with heavy boots and bare fists, in a climate which would kill most weaker men. Anyone who can terrorise such people must indeed be tough.

Zbszkos took some time to trace this superman. All that was known of him was that he had come to Alaska from Yugoslavia, that his name was Ivan Seric, and that his father and mother had been farmers. He was reputed to weigh only seventeen stone and measure six foot, but so terrific was his power that no man could even get his arm free once this Ivan Seric had grasped his wrist. It was said that he could lift the heaviest miner over his head with one hand and with a single movement. Some declared that he had strangled bears with his bare hands; others that he lifted rocks which no other man in all Alaska could move.

When Stanislaus caught up with Seric, he straight away took him into his private gym. Seric just grabbed the 24 stone, 5 ft 5 in Pole, former champion of the world, by each wrist and slowly forced him flat onto his back. Time 39 seconds. Then he did the same to Wladek. The utter amazement of the Zbyszko brothers can well be imagined. They had discovered their superman.

Moreover, Stanislaus soon found out that Seric was not like, say, former wrestler Primo Carnera, who knew little about boxing and only won the championship by the devastating power of his punches. The Alaskan was well versed in wrestling technique. However, Zbyszko also realised that a heavyweight as experienced and clever as Ed 'Strangler' Lewis might, in a 60 minute world title fight, take evading action and prevent Seric from getting to grips.

During my stay in America Zbyszko had constantly emphasised that super-strong men of little action, like Primo or Gama of India, Godfrey and Steinke, inevitably kill houses for boxing and wrestling.

Both wrestlers gave me their own versions of the controversial fight which took place in New York.

Lewis: 'I gave him nothing. After an hour we were still on our feet. He was far too strong to throw. The crowd was getting after us. I said, "Jack, one of us has got to retire or wrestling will be killed." He said, "If you give me six months to train for a return match I will retire."

'I gave the okay and he walked to his corner Jack: 'The guy wouldn't wrestle.'

The return match for the 'Overall World Heavyweight Championship': Ed 'Strangler' Lewis versus Jack Sherry, was billed to take place as Lewis had promised, six months later, in Philadelphia. Nearly every wrestler in America was there. But Lewis refused to wrestle.

Later, when Ed was wrestling for me in England, I asked him why.

'Cap, I guess it was like this. Jack never trained properly for our first match. He figured to put me down like he had everyone else. But I knew too much to let him come to grips. Naturally I could not do this a second time. When Jack came to Philadelphia he was in fine shape and had a man to help him. I couldn't fight two men at once. When I saw the second man standing behind Jack I knew I couldn't win so I let Sherry have the title.'

'Who was this other man whom you say Sherry brought along to help him beat you!' I asked.

'Father Time,' said Ed. 'One guy no one can beat!'

13. The World Beater Comes to Britain

I cabled Henri: 'Send him along', and Sherry duly arrived. I can honestly say that never before had I ever seen such a man. His physique was terrific. In order adequately to describe him, some comparison is needed. In England there was at that time a former British Amateur Welterweight Champion called Robert Cook, who weighed around 11 st 4 lbs and worked as a meat porter in Smithfield Market. His body was like an anatomical chart, used for teaching anatomy to medical students. He was said to be able to carry, on his shoulder, a half side of beef.

Sherry was moulded like Cook but on a vastly greater scale. At 17 1/2 stone he was far stronger than Bob. To us he looked like Hercules himself.

I decided to ask Gaston Gheveart, the new heavyweight champion of France (and strongest Frenchman after Charles Rigoulot) to come over and try out Sherry in the gym.

Gaston could lift well over 400 lbs above his head, using two hands. He stood five feet nine inches in height and tipped the scales at 19 st 9 lbs. He was a superlative wrestler at this time, and it was doubtful whether anyone in Europe could then beat him.

Gheveart, after a long train and boat journey from his home town the other side of Paris, arrived and stayed at my house. Sherry was booked into an hotel. I introduced Jack to Gaston, and then both stripped off for the test. This is what happened:

Round 1
Sherry walked over to Gaston and picked him up as if he had been a five-year-old. He held him for a second above his head, then put him down flat on his shoulders, holding him as in a vice for my count of three.
Time: 10 seconds.
'Formidable!' said Gheveart, looking astounded.

Round 2
Sherry again walked up to Gheveart, grabbed his wrist and using a double wrist lock, very slowly pinned him flat as a pancake.
Time: 23 seconds.
'Il est plus fort q'un cheval,' said Gaston.

Round 3
Sherry went for an ankle, upended Gheveart, and then clamped on a Japanese leg lock. Gaston instantly submitted.
Time: 23 seconds.

'C'est magnifique mais ce n'est pas la lutte,' gasped Gaston.

After this I had a long discussion with Gheveart. He maintained that, if the Americans could not match Sherry, how could we? Kathleen believed he was no showman and would 'kill' all houses, including Belle Vue.

We decided to consult the oracle and sent for Karl. Karl Pojello knew all about Sherry.

'Atol, I try out this man. Maybe you all scared. Zbyszko make big publicity. You no believe all you hear. 'But look what he did to Gheveart.'

'Gheveart amateur. He just weightlifter. Mr. Sherry no beat Mr. Pojello like that. All wrestlers beat weightlifters. Barbellers have veak necks. Atol, you beat Samson, strongest man in vorld, mit neck lock I tink. You know what I say true.'

But Sherry took Pojello with his double wrist lock. He forced this great champion's shoulders, in slow motion, down onto the mat. Karl, held as in a vice, could not move at all.

'Who else you got here!' growled Sherry in a voice more suited to the wide open spaces. A voice which could be heard all over the building and outside it.

'He very strong man. I fetch Mr. Bartush,' said Karl. Mr. Bartush, however, fared no better than his master.

'I tink, Atol, we have now greatest wrestler. Missis Look put him in Manchester. He draw big crowd. Everyone come see this man. You listen me. You make million dollars.'

All this was kept a dark secret. We knew that, if anyone found out the truth, Sherry's days as a wrestler would be numbered. No one in Europe would fight such a man.

One of the best European heavyweights was at that time resident in England. This was Guillaume Estelles, the 17 stone heavyweight champion of Switzerland. He worked as an engineer in London and was a naturalised British subject.

Guillaume was my height and had only lost on two occasions, once to Pojello and once to me. But when he was younger, neither I nor anyone else in England could beat him. He was as strong as, or stronger than, Gheveart. He was also a heavyweight of great experience and ability. Even Karl had taken three quarters of an hour to overcome him. Nor was there any waiting list among the Area Champions of Britain to take him on. So he was invariably matched against foreign champions. One cannot of course just match a world champion against anyone. But if he issues an open challenge then you must match him against whoever accepts, provided of course that the challenger is of reasonable ability.

We approached various leading British heavyweights to take on Sherry, but no one except that indomitable trio, Jack Pye, Norman the Butcher and Carver Doone, was particularly interested. We did not consider any of these three suitable for the debut in England of a champion who could pin Pojello and Gheveart as if they were novices. So we approached Estelles, who of course knew nothing of the trials, but, always supremely courageous, accepted the fight. Sherry startled Kathleen by demanding 20 per cent of the gate! Belle Vue was packed for the fight. Kathleen, radiant in a fabulous silver lame sheath dress covered in silver and gold sequins, made a short speech from the ring and shook hands with Guillaume and Sherry.

Then, as is the custom at such fights, various champions were introduced. Finally, the announcer, Tom Spedding, introduced the contestants. Sherry went over to him and muttered a few words.

Tom looked startled. Then he announced: 'Mr. Sherry wishes me to say that he offers ten thousand dollars to any judoist or boxer in the world who can stay 100 seconds with him.' You could literally hear the huge crowd gasp.

Jack had originally intended this '100 second challenge' (as it became known) to apply to all wrestlers. Pojello, however, had pointed out that if all the available heavyweight wrestlers were so bad that they could not last even two minutes, or Sherry was so good that they had no chance at all against him, then the British public would not pay to see him.

Then the fight began. It was a farce. Although asked to show some 'showmanship' Jack just shook hands with the Swiss and then put him straight down. Then he stood up, walked twice round the ring and double-wrist-locked Estelles. After holding the Swiss champion for three seconds, he got up and walked straight to his corner, put on his dressing gown and walked out to a storm of boos, cries, of 'fake', 'send him home' and so on.

Guillaume Estelles was always a popular favourite in England and particularly in Manchester. When a man of this calibre is put down like a baby in a few minutes, no one believes it. Only the amateur and professional wrestlers knew it was no fake. Even Bernard Gray said, 'Atholl, I am surprised at you. At least you could have arranged it better.'

Kathleen Look was in tears. She said to Sherry: 'Jack, you might have given him a short run. Even Hackenschmidt was said to have let his weaker opponents run for a few minutes. That is showmanship, not fake. Provided you do not lose, how can that be fake!'

'I don't know,' said Jack. 'All I know is you people can't wrestle.'

This fiasco very nearly killed not only Belle Vue but the whole wrestling scene. It opened wide the doors for many sports writers, who could not tell a wrestler from a geranium, to indulge in undiluted sarcasm.

But Pojello, Kathleen and I knew only too well that the fight was very far from being faked. To our chagrin we believed that we had been landed with a man whom we could not match and whom one and all would be afraid to meet. Two things might save us.

1. The 10,000 dollar challenge to the world's champion boxers must be put in writing. In this way, if any of them could last the 100 seconds, then he could legally enforce payment. You cannot bluff your way out of that sort of offer.

2. If Pojello or I could 'slow up' Jack. While no one suggested he should drop a fall or lose (everyone in USA knew he was incorruptible), surely he could go easy for a while? The old example: To win a mile do you have to go all out from the start? Does it matter how long you take so long as you win?

When I put argument to Jack he answered: 'Why should I amuse you people by fooling around for ten minutes when I can put anyone down in one minute? If you English cannot find me better opponents I might as well go back to Alaska where I can pick all the fights I need to keep in shape.

I replied, 'Mr. Sherry, let me make myself clear. Unless you do ease up I shall cancel your permit and send you back to South Africa.' Jack thought about this. Then he said:

'I don't know. — (another promoter) came to see me last night. He said, "Watch your step, this Oakeley is a son of a bitch. If you want a square deal you should appear for me."'

'What did you say to that?'

'I told him that I figured most guys, outside Alaska, were crooks. Every one wanted me to lose for some palooka. I don't lose for nobody in the world and nobody lives who can beat me.

'I don't ask or want you to lose. I spent my time, both as an amateur and a professional, trying to get fighters in England to win. Why should I want you to lose!'

'Maybe you don't, but others do. They make it a condition for some poor black man to come over, that he must lose or he won't get a permit to fight. What sort of a country has to give you a permit to fight? Is that how the British control challenges: no lose no permit? Is that the strength?'

'I do no such thing as to ask anyone to lose.'

'If that's so why do none of your big guys fight in America! We welcome everyone.'

'Lots do. I for one. Kid Berg and Jimmy Wilde both fought there and won.

'I never hoid of them.'

'How could you, out in the wilds?'

'Listen, Cap. Where I come from we don't figure on a lot of writing. Guy gives his word that's it. You give me your word you don't ever ask me to lose I make you right now my manager.

'I give my word.'

'Good. Now, how about a fall! I don't give no falls to anyone who can't take them and no one living can take a fall from me.

'You do not have to give any falls.'

'How about the referee? I must know who is to referee. In the States referees double cross, you know that.'

'No referee here will double-cross you, Jack.'

'Okay.

He shook my hand with a grip which nearly broke it,

'Now what you want me to do!'

Long hours I spent trying to teach this man showmanship. I taught him punishing holds to use before he brought in his finishing holds. But he never really learnt it. He used to ask:

'Why do I have to use a lot of holds when all I need to do is grab them and pin them!'

However, if he was a flop in his first match that was the first and last. By persistence and a tour of the provincial cities, we got the British public to appreciate his true worth. Instead of putting every one down in a minute we got him at least to take things easy. This, to Jack, meant bulling around till he got warm and then picking up his opponent above his head, swinging him round like a top and putting him down with a bang. At least this was a little more spectacular than straight away grabbing a man and putting him down in slow motion.

Each year, the 'Open to All Tournament", run by Miss Look, went from strength to strength. Heavyweights from all over the world entered—each year Jack Sherry defeated the winner. He never lost. He never refused a fight. He never dropped a fall.

Only two British heavyweight boxers, both of whom had fought in America, took up the challenge. Jack told them they could fight anyway they pleased with or without gloves. At Leicester, Reggie Meen pluckily lasted sixteen seconds. Then Phil Scott, a former British heavyweight champion, who had previously won an open British heavyweight tournament, accepted. Scott was strong, tall and heavy. People in England had underestimated him as a boxer but in my estimation he ranks with Tommy Farr as a far more formidable British champion than most of the lighter champions who came later. Admittedly he did not do so well in America, but this may well be because he had an English, not an American, manager in the States.

The fight was promoted by Victor Berliner at the Ring, Blackfriars. Sherry, supremely contemptuous of all heavyweights who had to wear gloves to fight, walked over and shook hands. He then held both arms above his head as if he was a prisoner surrendering;. Phil, like a flash, put in the most devastating punch I have ever seen. He struck Jack in the right groin with a blow which would have killed any other man. The Alaskan went down as if he had been poleaxed. All this happened in thirty seconds.

Phil (and everyone else) thought he had killed him. I must again impress on you that Scott was a giant of 6 ft 4 in and eighteen stone when he weighed in for this match.

For a few seconds Jack lay still. Then, slowly rising to his feet, he grabbed Scott's leg. Phil aimed another blow, but in a flash Sherry clamped on his deadly Japanese leg lock. In a second Phil was frantically shouting at the referee that he gave in. The time was just under the 100 seconds.

Jack, bent double, limped to the dressing room, where I saw him as he was attended by the doctor. The right side of his abdomen was horribly swollen with a huge black lump the size of a cricket ball. It looked to us as if the bowel had been ruptured.

'I guess you got one man over here who knows how to fight. What happened to him in the States?'

'You ought to know,' I said.

If Phil Scott ever reads this, let me say right now that he and Farr were the only English heavyweight champion boxers whom we wrestlers ever admired. Phil had all the courage, fighting spirit and guts to take on such a man as Jack Sherry. And if he failed in America at least he had the courage to go over and fight them on their own ground. Today only Cooper impresses me.

The swelling took a week to go down, but all was well that ended well and Jack recovered. For his courageous effort, which so nearly succeeded, Phil Scott was duly rewarded by the management.

After this Jack went to Turkey to fight the Turkish champion, a challenger for the world title. As everyone in wrestling knows, Turks are formidable matmen and this one was no exception.

Weighing around the twenty-eight stone mark, the challenger was expected by his own people—who did not know Sherry and thought American wrestling to be mainly fixed—to win easily over the American. The Turk however knew better than to imagine he was up against any kind of 'pushover'.

How much the Turkish champion knew about an episode which nearly ended the match before it had begun, we do not know Probably nothing. At any rate, with a hundred and twenty thousand people all waiting to see the match, a man came into the dressing room and asked Sherry through an interpreter if he would give him one fall in this 'best two out of three falls' match.

'Sure,' says Jack.

'When can he take it!' asked the man.

'When he can get it,' says Sherry. Upon which the man said a in of what sounded very much like Turkish swear words, and flew out of the room.

Jack went on undressing and thought no more about the incident

A few minutes later the same man returned and again asked Jack to give the champion a fall. Again Jack, this time annoyed, said 'No' in a way which left no doubt in the mind of the person concerned but that he meant what he said.

However he returned for the third time with two other men. They were all talking excitedly together.

They then came over and said that the Turk refused to wrestle! Eventually it was settled that Jack would wrestle one match in the Turkish style with one fall to decide. The Turk would then wrestle one fall in American Catch-as-Catch-Can style for the championship.

In the Turkish style, contestants wear heavy leather belts. Each man has to hold the other's belt, and whichever wrestler goes first to the ground loses the fall and the match. But whoever lets go the other's belt loses. This Turkish-style match took place before the world championship.

The Turk, being much the heavier, swung Jack around so hard that his own belt broke. Jack held it up to me and called out, loud as ever:

'Hey there—get this guy some new braces.'

Weight and skill in this style count far more than strength and Jack took seventeen minutes before he eventually threw the mammoth Turk. As he had never before even heard of the style, we thought that this was quite a feat.

In the title match Sherry pinned the challenger in 2 mins 25 seconds Despite the terrific strength of the Turk Jack handled him with ease.

'I could have done it sooner,' he said. 'I had to give them a good show.'

I thought, 'Two minutes twenty-five seconds to beat a challenger on his own territory and he calls that "a good show".'

One of the greatest drawing cards at Belle Vue was a huge giant named Sergei Kalmikoff, champion of Siberia. I had seen this man in America when he appeared at Madison Square Garden against Wladek Zbyszko. Like many educated Russians he was a marvellous actor with an ironic sense of humour. He was also a wrestler of terrific strength, and he combined this with such clever showmanship that everyone was convulsed with laughter.

I knew Sergei very well and liked him. After the Zbyszko match he promised to come to England, and as he was one of the highest paid heavyweights in America, and a drawing card second to none, this promise was one which I greatly appreciated.

Although people laughed at his antics, I never really believed that Kalmikoff was always trying to be funny. He was a very conceited man, a very good wrestler, and never liked being made to look foolish. But it was difficult to know just how much was real anger and how much was acting.

In the second minute of the American match Wladek tugged the Russian's beard and apparently pulled out a hair. Sergei, roaring with pain (which may or may not have been feigned), shook his fist at the Pole, walked straight to his corner and putting on his bath robe, stalked majestically out of the arena.

As he reached the exit he was confronted by some police who were on duty but watching the show. Sergei took one look at them, shouted 'Police' at the top of his voice, and tore back into the ring and began wrestling furiously.

He gave us a great deal of trouble on one occasion at Belle Vue. He was fighting King Curtis, who had heard all about the beard incident from me and had decided to do the same thing. It was a very rash move as Sergei, who weighed twenty-seven stone and had a twenty seven-inch neck and eighty-five-inch chest, was no sort of man to play tricks with.

However this magnificent showman at once repeated exactly what I had seen him do in America. He went to his corner, put on his dressing gown, and stormed out into the dressing room where he lay down full length on the couch and refused to go back despite all the efforts of Kathleen, myself, and Karloff Manoogian.

I can see him now with his immense body outstretched on the couch. He was nearly crying with apparent rage as he said: 'Poor Sergei. Sergei Russian gentleman. Capitalist Curtis make monkey out of great Russian gentleman. I think I kill him.' I said, 'Do what you like, Sergei, but for the love of mike go back and fight before the audience wreck the building.

He then started to weep in earnest saying: 'For forty-eight hours this great Russian gentleman stay in train to come to England for Mrs. Look. Then poor Russian gentleman take train to Manchester, more five hours. Seats for baby. Too small for poor Sergei. Can no go toilet. Toilet for babies. Poor Sergei can no go through door. Door for babies. Now Sergei wrestle at Belle Vue one minute. Then he go back again five hours and then again forty-eight hours in train to Russia. No good. I go home now.

Sergei cried and cried then he suddenly sat up, all smiles: 'How much extra you big capitalist Oakeley pay if I: go back!' 'Twenty-five pounds,' I said. At once he leapt to his feet and ran into the arena, climbed into the ring, pinned King in a minute or so and then came charging back. 'Where do we eat!' he asked.

On another occasion, in London, I wanted Sergei to give me an option on his services. Unfortunately Boganski and Manoogian, who were acting as interpreters, told me that there was no word in Russian for 'option'.

with Sergei lying on his bed, we three tried for hours to make him understand. Finally I asked Karloff to put it this way: 'On the first of January you get a letter from Mr. Bankier and one from me. Both ask you to wrestle in England but I have the option. For whom do you come!' Sergei sat up all smiles. 'Nine hours Oakeley and you yap yap yap. Nine hours poor Sergei listen but no understand. Now I understand. Mr. Bankier write Sergei and Mr. Oakeley write Sergei. For whom Sergei wrestle! Easy. For whoever pays ze most monie. Now all go away and let poor Sergei sleep.' So we gave up the fight and left him to sleep.

One day the owner of the hotel said: 'Mr. Oakeley, I cannot have Mr. Kalmikoff taking a bath with the door open and all the water pouring down the staircase.'

I saw Sergei and told him what the owner had said.

'What can poor Sergei do,' he replied. 'Bath for baby; bathroom for babies. Sergei get into room no can get into bath. Door will no shut. Sergei get in bath and all water leave bath and go down the stairs. Everything in England only for babies, not for Russian gentleman.'

Poor Sergei left us and we never saw him again. He was shot when the Germans invaded Russia.

14. Wrestlers at Work - and at Play

Although, as I have said, Jack's appearances at Belle Vue always attracted a capacity house (at double prices), it was some time before the knowledgeable wrestling audiences of the North realised that here was the Master Matman.

Then Sherry beat the world heavyweight champion (Cumberland and Westmorland style) without apparent effort. The ease with which Jack had handled this man, eighteen stone Douglas Clark of Huddersfield, exemplified his terrific strength. Douglas, who was well known as a first-class rugger player, as well as being open champion at the Grasmere Games, was a very powerful athlete. Although he had failed to defeat me he had beaten other British heavyweights from the South in a matter of minutes. By trade he was a coal merchant, and once told me that he kept up his strength by carrying and delivering his sacks of coal.

It was this victory that convinced every journalist north of Birmingham that Sherry was a wrestler and fighter greater than anyone they had seen before. This view was also held by George Hackenschmidt, himself one of the greatest and strongest heavyweights at the time of Stanislaus Zbyszko, Frank Gotch and the great Russian champion, Padoubney.

Thus when Jack was called upon each year to meet the winner of the great 'no one barred' international eliminating tournaments for the world title, it was small wonder that those able to obtain tickets considered themselves lucky.

Sherry of course reigned supreme in these finals. Even Kola Kwariani, the great White Russian champion, did not bother him. When one considered Kola was entered by the 'opposition' in USA to demolish Sherry and won the Eliminating Tournament for the last year before the war, yet still failed even to get a single fall from the mat master, Sherry's fantastic strength can be appreciated. I reckoned Kola and Zelezniak to be twice as strong as both Douglas and George Clark (the Highland Games Hercules and record holder) yet Sherry handled Kwariani as a master teaching a pupil, and without exerting himself at all.

Jack's colossal force, voice, and direct way of speaking always amused us. He never tried to be funny but often succeeded unintentionally.

One night at Belle Vue before the preliminaries began Kathleen Went over to Jack and said, 'The directors have asked to see me. Would you look after the front of the house for a few minutes while I'm away!'

'Sure thing, Kay,' says Jack.

Twenty minutes later Kathleen in tears came to see me. 'Really, Atholl, it's too bad. One of my best customers brought a journalist and they say Jack insulted them.'

I called Jack and he strolled over.

'What's up Cap! You lookin' fierce.'

I faced him with Kathleen and the journalist, who said, 'We were ushered in but given seats behind one of the iron pillars. Mr. Sherry came over and was rude to us.'

'What happened, Jack?'

'Oh, nothing much. These two little guys bellyached to me they had been seated behind a pillar. I said, "What the hell you want me to do, move the pillar!"'

'Jack,' says Kay, 'you really are impossible. Did you honestly believe they wanted a Samson act!'

'Samson wasn't all that strong,' retorted Jack as he walked off.

During this period Kathleen Look had been asked to promote the open 'Championship of the World' tournament in Austria. Jack said he might get cold 'standing around to meet the winner' so it was arranged he would wrestle according to the draw. No one was seeded.

The tournament was to be held at the Engelmann Arena in Vienna. Kathleen had not been abroad before and both her mother and father were apprehensive at her travelling alone by train on such a long journey.

Karl assured her parents that he would see their daughter was adequately protected. When I arrived in Vienna, Kay told me: 'Atholl, it was quite fantastic. Karl saw me off at Victoria and gave me such a huge bunch of flowers that I felt like a prima donna. Two more wrestlers met me at Dover and saw me onto the boat. At Calais two huge French heavyweights met me with more flowers! They saw me onto the train, where I had a First Class reservation. Then two Americans met me in Paris, and took me out to dinner (and more flowers). At last they put me on the train for Vienna and here I am!'

The Engelmann was very big tournament. It went on every night for a month with an average nightly attendance of over eleven thousand.

Meanwhile, Jack and I had been hitting it up with Dick Shikat and Kola Kwariani in Paris for a week, after which both of us were the worse for wear. Having told us that Stalin could still stand up after drinking thirteen Russian Vodkas, Kwariani said that he could manage seven, and challenged Jack to outdrink him

Jack, who never even contemplated the possibility of being beaten at anything, at once accepted. I sat next to him. Halfway through dinner the waiter poured me out a glass about the size of a thimble. Having been forewarned I drank only a sip and, when he was looking the other way, poured the other half into Sherry's glass. Kwariani then gave a toast: 'Here's to world sport. May it always remain nonpolitical!'

Jack dashed down his Vodka, stood up, and with a resounding crash fell under the table. 'There goes the Champ,' drawled Kola, resplendent in full Cossack uniform.

We left Jack there for the rest of the dinner. Eventually he regained consciousness and the rest of the night was spent going round all the night clubs in Paris, under Kwariani's direction.

When Jack and I returned to the hotel Karloff Manoogian was shaving.

'Where you guys been all night!' he asked.

'How do I know,' says Sherry. 'Someone fixed my drink.'

In consequence Jack was not in the best of shape. In fact we all had a fright when, in the first round of the tournament, Michel Leoni, the Italian champion and another protege of Pojello's, looked at one time like dethroning him. However Jack, with tears streaming down his face, pulled himself together and clamped on his double wrist lock in the third round.

But he was very shaken, and spent all the next week sitting by himself' in the Bier Garten drinking milk in between vicious workouts in the local gym.

Of all the fights, that between Mike Brendel (Hungarian champion) and Karloff Manoogian (Armenian/Syrian champion) was the most vicious. They hated each other like poison. Brendel got Manoogian in a short-arm scissors and then drove the point of his elbow with immense force into the Armenian's stomach.

Late that night Jack and I found Manoogian hiding behind a curtain in the hotel. Sherry asked him what he was doing. 'Waiting for that son of a bitch Brendel,' says Karloff. Sherry grabbed him and found, strapped to his leg, a fearful looking Turkish-style knife. After much persuasion, but without using force, Sherry manoeuvred Manoogian back to his room. We met Mike outside and sent him to another hotel. In the morning we learnt that Karloff, now out of the tournament, had left for Paris. In his room we found all the sheets and all the curtains cut to ribbons by that terrible knife! Jack said, 'I guess it was a good idea sending that Brendel some place else.'

The only British wrestler to enter this tournament was a certain 'Gentleman Jim', a heavyweight very popular with continental crowds. Jim was in top form and fought his way into the semi-finals —no mean achievement when you consider that most of the world's best heavyweights were in this tournament.

One morning a seven-foot-high Austrian with a massive beard came to the hotel. Under the Austrian hat (with a shaving brush) he looked enormous. 'I vant to see Gentleman Jim.' He looked so fierce that we decided to escort him to Jim's bedroom in case of trouble. Jim visibly blanched when we entered his room.

You Gentleman Jim!' asked the Austrian.

'Yes,' said Jim, looking apprehensive.

'You take my wife to night club last night?'

'I didn't know she was your wife', stammered Jim. 'I am very sorry.

'Vot for are you sorry? In Austria husbands are not selfish. When we are busy we do not try to stop our wives having good time. We trust them. When we work late it is custom for them to be escorted by our friends.'

Jim breathed again. The Austrian took out his wallet. At first Jim thought he was pulling a gun, but instead he handed the Englishman a wad of notes.

'What's this for!' asked Jim.

'In Austria it is the custom for a husband to make sure that his wife's escort is not put to any expense. Good morning, sir, and thank you.'

He shook hands all round and left. Everyone gave an audible sigh of relief. You see, Jack Sherry had gone out early that morning for road work. The huge Austrian reminded me of Mike Romano's story about his giant Texan.

Of course Sherry won the tournament. They were wonderful weeks and we all had a marvellous time in Vienna. One Sunday night Jack was sitting in the Bier Garden. Lovers everywhere were under the trees, and romantic as anyone could have wished for. A violinist came over and played Strauss to him.

'Wonderful place Vienna, Jack,' I said.

'Okay if you're in love,' says Jack. 'I gotta wife in New York.'

'I didn't know that.'

'Yeah, I got hooked before I left.'

'Does she write to you?'

'Nope. I forgot to tell her where I was going.'

'Do you mean to say you just left and never told her you were going to South Africa!'

'I just told you. I forgot.'

Jack went back to America three years later. When he later returned to England he told me, 'My wife and I broke up.' 'Why!' I asked.

'I went along to my apartment and let myself in with my key. After a while in comes a young boy. He looks at me and calls out, "Hey, Mom, there's a strange man in the joint."

'My wife says, "Where you been all this time!"

'I told her, "England."

'She asks me, "Why didn't you say you was going away!"

'"I forgot."

'"You been away three years. Why didn't you write?"

'"I sent you regular money. I don't write much."

'"You don't write at all."

'"Who's the boy?"

'"That's your son."'

I asked Jack why she left him.

'I guess she got bored without me,' says Jack, 'and found herself another guy.'

Years later Jack remarried. He gave me a picture of himself with his bride, a beautiful Yugoslav girl. She presented him with a son and daughter about whom he never tired of writing to me.

The wrestling promoter at the Liverpool Stadium was William Bankier, ex-world famous Scottish strong man in earlier days. I liked Bill, who had once been the promoter in a bout I had fought with

Rene Norris, an Australian. Carver and I had also wrestled against opponents chosen by him at the Tower, Blackpool.

Bulldog Bill Garnon, after three years in America, had now returned to England. As far as British heavyweights were concerned he was now in a class by himself. Having been sparring partner to the best American heavyweights, what he did not know about wrestling was not worth knowing. A man of indomitable courage and as dogged as they come, the Weighs Bulldog challenged Sherry.

Kathleen promoted this match as an open-air contest in Liverpool.

Whether he was egged on by the press to (expose the fraud' may ever be known, but Bankier put on the Liverpool Stadium programme that if this match was for the world's heavyweight wrestling championship then sixpence was all that it was worth. He used the word 'Mongolian' in regard to Sherry.

Although I had, for some time, been watching for any statement that Sherry was not champion, I never expected Bill Bankier to disparage a heavyweight whom, as an expert he knew, or should have known, was all that he claimed to be.

The programme was handed me by a Belle Vue fan. I showed it to Sherry who was livid with rage, not at the '6d' but because of the insinuation that he was a Mongolian! We went to my solicitors and Jack was advised that, though 'Mongolian' was not defamatory, the way in which his world championship had been related to a sixpence undoubtedly was.

Writs, on behalf of Sherry and Garnon, were issued for libel. To my certain knowledge every effort was made to get Sherry to call off his action. A leading heavyweight even came over from America and tried for hours to convince Jack that he should settle. The case was heard in the High Court in Liverpool with Maxwell Fyfe leading for the plaintiffs. Jack came into court in a 'pepper-and salt' suit which the solicitors sent him out to change. When Sherry returned the judge had already entered. Jack took one look at the numerous legal gentlemen, all arrayed in their wigs, and boomed in his thunderous voice:

'Say, why has Bankier got all these guys when I've only got one?'

After listening to the three-hour cross-examination of Sherry the judge in his summing up said that he had listened to the answers of Mr. Sherry and that, in his view, Mr. Sherry was all that he claimed to be.

It was in this case that evidence, brought over from America, proved beyond all doubt that Sherry was the overall heavyweight wrestling champion of the world and both Jack and Bill Garnon were awarded substantial damages and costs.

This case, unique in the annals of sport, dumbfounded all the 'knockers' here and in the States. An Australian paper, widely circulated, printed a long article in praise of Sherry's honesty as a wrestler.

Soon after this case I noticed a press report suggesting that a match between two named heavyweights, one of whom was under contract to us, had been a pre-arranged fight. I knew for certain that this fight was in no way fixed so I advised both fighters that they should sue. This they did and their honesty was upheld.

The final Sherry episode occurred before he left for America, when he suddenly got an appendicitis. Though in agony he refused to see a doctor. 'I need some wine,' he said. This was at a time when he had arranged a farewell dinner for Kathleen and myself in honour of what he imagined we had done for him.

Nothing small about Jack. Everything had to be on a grand scale. We had a corner table, and he ordered seven bottles of wine, insisting that they should all be put on the table at once. He drank most of them himself and did not notice Kathleen pouring her often filled glass into a plant pot. After drinking a bottle, I poured the contents of my glass into that of Kathleen. We reckoned Jack drank five bottles, that night, and still remained sober. Of course it did him no good so the next day I got a taxi and took him to Dr. Grainger, who diagnosed acute appendicitis.

Under protest he allowed us to take him to the7 Middlesex Hospital. Here he agreed to be operated on but only if he was given a local anaesthetic—not gas—and allowed to watch the proceedings. I asked him why he objected to a general anaesthetic.

'I got to see they don't cut my stomach muscle so I can't wrestle no more.

'Why should they want to do that!'

'How do I know! Bankier might pay them to put me out of business.'

I saw the house surgeon. He said, 'leave it to me.'

As I said goodbye I saw a priest at Jack's bedside, giving him the last rites. Sherry had never before had a day's illness. To him this was the end.

The next morning I went to the hospital. The surgeons, roaring with laughter, took me to their private room.

'What happened!' I asked.

'Well,' replied one of the surgeons, 'he would not let us anaesthetise him and insisted on watching us. So we rigged a mirror and gave him a prick in his back as he had asked for a spinal anaesthetic. I then made a minute scratch on his stomach. He fainted at once so we slapped the mask over his face, gave the anaesthetic in the normal way, and proceeded with the operation. But unfortunately we could not remove the appendix as he had peritonitis and we had to drain it. He will have to have it removed in America. Perhaps you will tell him?'

I went in to Jack. There was no sign of him. Only smoke coming out of the bed. The sister pulled back the bedclothes. 'I told you you could not smoke, Mr. Sherry. Please do as I ask you.'

Jack put the cigarette out and said: 'I had Charlie Manoogian in here this morning. He frightened all the nurses and brought me a lousy big bunch of flowers. I said, "What the hell you bring these for—I'm not dead?" '

'Where are the flowers?' I asked.

'I threw 'em out of the window,' says Jack.

'And I went down and picked them up,' said his nurse.

Jack made no comment when I told him he would have to be operated on again in America. The sister told me he was the worst patient she had ever nursed.

'He won't lie on his back and he gets out of bed to turn over in case his shoulders touch,' she said.

Jack left for America in 1939. At the ship we shook hands. He said, 'When I arrived here they told me you were a son of a bitch, but poisonally I found you a hundred poicent.'

I never saw him again although he wrote regularly. He died in 1969—aged 75 but looking 40—from what his daughter described as a 'massive heart attack'. Even at the end he had to go out like a lion. Jack Sherry was a very great man, undoubtedly the greatest and strongest fighter of modern times.

15. A Muddy Interlude

'How do Indians wrestle in India?' I asked Karl one day.
'Vot you mean, how Indians wrestle!' He looked puzzled. 'What do they wrestle on—mats?'
'No. No mats. Just earth. Very good, very soft. I like very much wrestle on soft earth like Indian champions.'
This conversation set me thinking. When I returned to England I went down to the Blackfriars Ring to see my friend and co-promoter, Victor Berliner.
'Victor, I have an idea. A joke which may well be the funniest ever played on London.' 'What sort of a joke?'
I told him about the conversation with Pojello.
'I'm sorry,' he said, 'but I don't follow you, Atholl.'
'Well, it's like this. Pojello, as you know, is a serious champion. He says he would like to wrestle on earth. Why don't we let him!'
'What, fill the ring with earth!'
'We'll tell Karl it's earth but in reality...'
'In reality what?'
'We'll put down clay and cover it in oil. Neither wrestler will be able to stand up. When they enter the ring they will slip all over the place. It should be quite amusing.'
'Atholl, I'm afraid you have a sardonic sense of humour. What happens if Pojello realises such a mess is not the sort of earth he expected!'
'Karl is in Paris. He won't arrive until Thursday afternoon. I'll bring him to the Ring about 9 pm. Up to then the ring will have the mat down. The mud mixture, in drums, can be laid during the interval, after we have taken of the mats. Karl won't know anything about it until he enters the ring. We'll camouflage the mixture to look like earth. I'll tell Karl that we have put earth down so that he could wrestle a match on earth like the Indians. It should be a riot.'
Believe you me, dear reader, it most certainly was. London rocked under the impact. The Daily Mirror printed a picture right across its front page. The press turned up by the hundred. People fought to get in. Never was there such a spoof, never such a revoltingly funny spectacle. Press and public fell for it hook, line and sinker. Never before, or since, have people laughed as they did that

first night at what Victor and I advertised as 'The World Premiere of Mud Wrestling'.

But the real point of the joke was that neither Pojello nor his opponent, Bulldog Bill Garnon, nor even the referee, Phil Meader, had been told anything about the frame-up.

Of course they knew that we were using earth, but they naturally thought it would be dry, clean earth. In fact it was nothing of the sort. Victor sent out a squad of men to dig up and bring back clay in forty-gallon drums. Over a ton arrived. This was followed by a forty-gallon drum of lubricating oil, Castrol. To make the earth look dark we obtained three sacks of soot.

No one, except Victor and me, knew a thing about it. The men who brought the clay never saw the men who brought the oil. Those who brought the oil never saw those who brought the clay. And the soot Victor obtained privately from a chimney sweep.

Victor supervised the preliminaries. The Blackfriars Ring had been sold out for days, for our publicity agent had whispered around that something was in the wind. Curiosity filled the stadium.

I brought in Karl just before the interval. The mats were still down as we walked into the dressing rooms. Garnon was already there. Then the interval was announced and referee Meader joined us.

I said: 'We are trying out earth instead of a mat. Karl says it's softer. If the experiment is successful we can save ourselves the expense of buying mats at £100 a time.'

Phil was immaculate in white flannels. Garnon wore black shorts. Karl long white wrestling tights.

Inside the stadium thirty men were emptying clay and spreading it out over the ring, where foot-high boards prevented it from falling out. The top of the concoction was level with the top of the boards. There was a buzz of amazement when the forty gallons of oil was poured all over the clay. But when the bags of soot were brought in everyone suddenly realised what was going on, and there was a roar of laughter which well-nigh took off the roof.

Back in the dressing room Karl, beaming all over his face, said: 'Ve make good match. Mr. Bulldog Garnon now top-class wrestler. He learn much in America. I no take him lightly. You all see good fight between two very serious, honest men. I say only best man vin. I try very hard be that best man. You see.'

'Doesn't look much like earth to me,' said Bill as he passed me. 'Too durned black to be earth.'

He swung over the ropes, landed on his feet and immediately slid out, head first, into the ringside seats. He clambered back and, holding onto the two top ropes, stood upright in his corner.

I was standing near when he leaned over and said, 'look you, Atholl, I don't think this funny whatever.'

I replied, 'You look like a chimney sweep.'

The whole audience were having hysterics. Tears rolled down their faces. Victor's man chose this opportunity to sell 9d paper mackintoshes to people in the ringside seats.

Then Karl came in. Smiling imperturbably, and looking more dignified (if possible) than ever, he stepped between the ropes, took three steps forward, fell flat on his face, and shot out of the ring like someone on the Cresta Run.

The people, tears streaming down their faces, rocked with laughter.

Then came Phil Meader. He also stepped in and went out as if shot from a bow.

I can truthfully say that I have never seen people so convulsed as were all those spectators that night. Mud was all over the place. The three in the ring looked like gollywogs. The ringsiders looked as if they had been riding to hounds on a wet day.

Karl leaned over and angrily called out, 'Atol, you play big joke on me. I tink not so funny. I gree wrestle like Indian. Not like water buffalo. I tink I give you good prescription ven I come out.'

The 'match' (if you could call it that) was deadly serious—which was what made it so fantastically funny. Every time one wrestler picked up the other, the whole lot collapsed in a sea of mud and oil and went shooting out of the ring. After ten minutes all the front-row people looked as if they had been in a rugger scrum. Six people in the circle had to be treated for acute hysterics, and one man had an epileptic fit.

So did we the next morning when we received the cleaners' bills for mud-covered dresses and dinner-jackets. We had to pay £186 to replace one lady's dress which had been so saturated with soot and oil that it was uncleanable.

One journalist who had got a slab of mud in his eye was not amused when a wrestler in the press room handed him a whisky and said: 'Here's mud in your eye.'

'Bottoms up,' said another pressman to Phil Meader.

Another ingenious journalist, for once unable to find anything in the wrestling on which to exercise his sarcasm, wrote that the clay had been dug up from a nearby graveyard. Someone else wrote. 'the contestants were oiI at sea), and no one could deny but that night even our great champions had feet of clay.

Victor was not slow to see the financial value of such entertainment. He decided, against my advice, to put it on again the following Thursday. While it is true that within twenty-four hours of its announcement every seat in the house was again sold, this time at triple prices, the second week was an anti-climax.

The initial show had only been so hilarious because first, no one had any idea of what was going to happen"—they thought it was to be a new sort of wrestling. And secondly, because Karl Pojello was in deadly earnest. With his high domed head he looked like a nuclear physicist on the moon, but he was extremely angry at the trick. So was Garnon, usually a most placid man.

Also, the angrier the contestants became, the funnier it all looked. Every time either took a hold, he slipped and skedaddled as if on a toboggan into the audience. Once all three went out and fell in a heap on the floor. Soon the contestants, the referee, the seconds, and most of the ringsiders looked like Jim Wango. If you can imagine motor oil and soot mixed you should be able to imagine what they all looked like. Although we advertised it as mud' everyone believed this to be a joke and that it was really ordinary earth as in India. In the second show both British wrestlers larked about. We were not allowed to use soot or oil. Everyone laughed politely, but the roar that goes up from a crowd when something really funny happens was absent. No one had hysterics.

Having livened the fighting scene by giving the British public something to laugh about, we went back to the serious business of wrestling. But Karl still had to be appeased. His sense of humour had been overstretched. He was a serious professional athlete, respected and renowned throughout the world, and he felt he had been made into a buffoon. But he was too good-natured to bear malice. After two days together in Paris we were once again the best of friends.

It is at this stage that something happened which made Karl a millionaire. But for the war and my misplaced sense of duty it would have made me one as well. Not that money meant much to me. As the chief contact for Sir Charles Higham I had been a highly paid man in advertising, and money from my American tour and all our promotions had been pouring in. I had a 100 mph eightcylinder car and (what was far more important) supreme strength and health, together with true friends of almost every nationality and all over the world.

Pojello and Sherry were both religious men. Not perhaps so much in the sense of the Church but in the sense of the teaching of Jesus of Nazareth. No one ever asked either of these two for assistance without getting it. The same went for Karloff Manoogian. As far as these three were concerned the parable of the good Samaritan had not fallen on deaf ears.

One sunny spring evening, Karl and I were sauntering down the Boulevard des Italiens when suddenly he said, 'Atol. You see vot I see?'

There coming towards us was a poor man. He was in rags, one boot was missing, he had no socks. But that was not all. As my eyes took him in I felt the hair rising on the nape of my neck. I felt I was looking at something from another age—a prehistoric monster. If I had met Pithecanthropus himself, in a fashionable Paris boulevard, I could not have been more astounded. What I saw coming towards us was utterly frightful. It was monstrous, unbelievable.

No human being I had ever seen had looked like this creature, ambling along like a grotesque ape. Its over-long arms trailed down by its knees; its fingers were bigger than bananas; its wrists carved inwards and, accentuated by the shrunken sleeves, were thicker than a man's ankles. The width of its shoulders was three times that of any normal man, yet the thing was shorter in stature than either Karl or myself. I felt absolutely aghast and horrified. Then I saw its face. I felt faint, and saw that Karl too had gone as white as a sheet.

The thing's head war longer from forehead to chin than that of a horse. Its hairless skull had a serrated crack down the middle, stretching from forehead to crown.

In Paris, especially at night, destitute people, some like bundles of rags, can be seen huddled against walls. I thought, Lon Chaney in the Hunchback of Notre Dame was Errol Flynn compared with this terrible thing.'

The creature, whatever it was, shuffled by, looking neither to left nor to right. Karl said, 'Atol, I go see. I no like zat poor zing.'

I think that very few people would have acted as Karl did. The creature was revolting, bizarre, inhuman, horrifying. And in addition I felt it was menacing. But Pojello went after it in a flash. I saw him apparently talking7 to it and gesticulating, while the monster stood still, not moving. I was standing a few feet behind it and facing Karl. I heard him speak in English, French, German, Italian and Spanish. Still the monster stood like a ghoul. Then I heard Karl say something in some other language (afterwards he told me it was Russian).

Instantly this terrible creature, weeping like a babe, was in his arms. 'Atol, quick, you help me please. Zis zick man. Very zick man. Quick. Quick!!'

I took one fantastic arm. It felt like a leg. We helped the creature into a little car, and then after a meal and hot coffee we heard a fantastic story.

But first I should explain how a human being could be physically transformed in this way. Bodily growth is governed by a gland called the pituitary. Should this gland become over-active before the age of sixteen, the frontal bones of the face become prominent and a man grows into a giant. All men over seven foot in height are 'pituitary giants' and are easily recognisable as such.

But if the pituitary gland suddenly becomes over-active after the age of sixteen (or thereabouts) the result is acromegalian, or a kind of giant dwarf. The bones swell; the head and body vastly increasing in size. But the legs do not grow and remain out of proportion. The additional weight of this huge body is too much for the legs, which cannot carry so heavy a load. Therefore, almost without exception, acromegalians are invalids usually confined to a wheel chair.

Karl found out that this man was an acromegalian. His father had been a Russian officer, killed by the Germans. His mother a head mistress of a girls' school in - (I do not wish to identify the town.)

But in one way our monster was unique. Acromegaly is often a killer before really monstrous deformities appear. Yet every day this man was becoming bigger and bigger, and more and more deformed.

Whereas no other acromegalian, in the history of medical science, had ever been known to Possess legs strong enough to enable him to fight, the legs of this man had been artificially developed to meet the strain of his mighty torso.

He told Karl that he had been in the Submarine Service at the time the acromegaly started. They had discharged him, and he had lived by doing odd jobs at night. He had had no food for over a week when we met him, and he was starving.

I couldn't understand his French but Karl made himself understood in Russian. As usual Pojello was brimming over with optimism and enthusiasm. 'Atol, I make zis man million dollars. No vun in world like him. I teach him wrestling.'

Frankly my English education, schoolmasters and others had never prepared me for such a situation. I saw at once that this man must be very strong. One had only to look at his hands, wrists and fingers. He placed one hand like a whole bunch of bananas over mine. Beneath it mine disappeared. He squeezed it gently, his eyes still full of tears. We understood one another although we could not communicate. Poor, poor man. I could have wept to see how harshly he had been treated.

I have set down these facts in some detail in order to show you what a fantastic character this Pojello was: brilliantly clever, generous, good-natured, kind and superlatively polite. I know of no other man in Karl's walk of life who would have stopped to help such a terribly deformed creature. To quote Jack Sherry who said bluntly, 'I guess he did what Christ told him to do and it paid off.'

Well, it certainly did 'pay off', as you will see. When Karl spoke to the monster he was moved by pity, not gain. If anyone had told either of us then that this poor thing was a walking gold mine, we would have laughed ourselves silly.

'Ask him if he knows any English,' I said.

Karl said something in Russian to the monster, who pointed at Karl and said, 'Angel'.

So we called him 'the Angel.'

16. Angel: The Sawn-off Giant

Karl took a whole year to train our 'Angel', and the training went on for nine hours each day. It took place in Paris under the strictest secrecy with no one but Karl and me knowing anything about it. Pojello never let our protege out of his sight. They shared a room over the gym and only went out at night, and they ate all meals in their room.

Under Pojello's tuition the Angel (whose real name was Maurice Tillett) slowly learned to wrestle. I have often been asked, since Maurice (after Sherry's retirement undefeated) subsequently won the world's heavyweight championship, as to who was the stronger of these two champions.

This kind of question is similar to asking which is the heavier—a ton of feathers or a ton of lead! The one is avoirdupois, the other troy. Angel was what Jack called a 'sawn-off-giant. But Sherry was always the real giant.

While Sherry was a herculean, seventeen stone six-footer, finely trained without an ounce of fat, Angel was over twenty-four stone but only five foot six inches in height. Unlike Sherry he had the long arms, massive trapezius and heavy stomach of the male gorilla. His whole body was completely covered, back and front, with long black hair.

In wrestling positions Sherry was able through his vast strength to exert far greater leverage than the shorter man. Angel, despite his arms, which were long only in relation to his body, had no such leverage to exert.

Sherry always grabbed a wrist or a leg and, by fantastic force, levered his opponent over. Once Sherry took hold of anyone's wrist escape was impossible. Nor could anyone even begin to resist the terrific leverage he used to turn over an opponent.

Angel was taught by Karl to force his way in, encircle his opponent's waist and break in his ribs with one crushing 'bear-hug'. While there was no escape from Sherry's wrist and leg locks, there was no escape once Angel got his long hairy arms round anyone.

Sherry of course was by far the better wrestler. He had had years and years of experience. Since he was a nine-year-old boy he had been a fanatic for fitness. Angel was sick, ill and starving when we found him. It took all of three months before he recovered his strength. His legs had been fast deteriorating. Only Karl's combined knowledge of advanced physical culture and orthopaedics saved the legs from complete deterioration. When we first met Maurice he could hardly walk. After three months with Karl he was doing a hundred full knee bends. In a year he could do a thousand non-stop.

Angel treated Karl as a stray starving dog would treat a master who had rescued him from vivisection. His instinct was to do whatever his benefactor asked him, without counting the cost. He neither argued nor protested, but recognised Pojello as a genius and acted accordingly. Me he regarded as his co-benefactor, someone who would promote his first public appearances.

Maurice Tillet, an Acromegalian, discovered, and trained by Pojello and the author and named by them 'The Angel'.

Karl decided that, once seen, every manager in the world, every circus owner and every wrestling promoter would make a bee line to sign up our Angel. Accordingly I had a contract drawn up by which Pojello and I together took fifty per cent and Angel the other fifty. Karl needed my knowledge of British advertising and promotion to put him over.

The one question mark was Kathleen Look's reaction: would she agree to Promote a monstrosity with a face two feet long?

'I tink Missis Look like better the Marquis of Gardiazabel than our Angel,' said Karl rather sadly. The elegant Marquis was six foot four and a very good-looking man. He was Kay's find, the winner of a Spanish tournament. He was a real marquis and one of her star attractions at Belle Vue, Manchester.

We decided to bring Angel to England by night. I told the proprietor of a small hotel that he was in a circus. But I took care to ensure that the proprietor did not see him in person.

Our next move was to arrange for Kathleen to meet him. We hired a private room and sent her an invitation. Kathleen, dressed to kill, and looking as always supremely glamorous, came into the room. Angel rose to meet her and she dropped like a stone.

After we had carried her into the manager's office we found it quite impossible to persuade her to return to our room.

'You must be off your heads to put that thing into wrestling,' she gasped. 'It's intolerable. Don't expect me to have anything to do with it.'

Privately she said, 'Atholl, please have nothing to do with this. It's too frightful for words. Pojello's gone mad. The thing is quite inhuman. What on earth are you going to do if it gets out of control! You might as well bring in an ape from the zoo. I think it is too terrible for words. I feel absolutely sick. It could quite easily give a pregnant woman a miscarriage.'

Having failed to win Kathleen over to our side I decided to 'go it alone'. Being well in with my Nottingham promoter I explained that the Angel was a 'rather fearsome object'. But of course I avoided any indication of what I was really going to show the public.

However my advertisements announced that a 'monster' as terrible in appearance as Neanderthal man would appear. I wrote all the publicity and minced no words. No one really believed it but the advertisements raised curiosity and people began to talk.

On the night of the fight, Angel was brought in a darkened car, and taken into a private dressing room. No one saw him. I looked outside and saw an enormous queue. We estimated there were over twenty thousand people waiting to buy tickets.

Angel's opponent was first sent into the ring. Then Karl brought in the Angel. The effect as he entered was absolutely electrifying. There was a colossal gasp from the audience, then, together like soldiers on parade, five women in the ringside seats all toppled over sideways together to the left. We saw other women fainting all over the hall. Never have I heard such language as some of the men in the audience used that night. From all over the stadium one heard shouts of, 'What the bloody hell is it?' 'Where the hell did you dig that thing up, Atholl!'

It is not my intention to pour out superlatives in connection with Angel's ring appearances. Caring nothing for bare-knuckle blows which his opponent rained on his monstrous horse-face, Maurice closed at once. Locking his great long hairy arms around his opponent, he crushed him.

Angel had only a few fights in England. In one of these the great Karl Reginsky, a Belle Vue star, and hardest hitting fighter in the world, covered Maurice's face in blood. Angel looked like a butcher's nightmare, or something out of Dante's Inferno.

In Manchester at the Free Trade Hall, a crowd estimated by the police at 30,000 gathered outside. Suddenly the Hall was rushed. The main staircase to the balcony was blocked solid by a shouting, milling crowd. The stewards were swept off their feet and the situation became extremely ugly.

Karl Reginsky, whose courage, determination and fighting ability had made him a prime favourite with the tough, down-to-earth Manchester audiences, stormed to the top of the staircase. Wearing only his scarlet and black wrestling shorts, the shaven-headed Reginsky stood like Horatius defending the bridge, his golden brown muscles rippling as he faced the leaders.

I heard him call: 'The first man who moves another step and I pick him up and throw him back over your heads.'

Arms folded, Reginsky reminded me of a Greek god. A single light picked him out, while the crowd were in semi-darkness.

I heard the word passed back: 'Reginsky is at the top of the stairs. Go on back chaps before someone gets hurt.'

Slowly the crowd withdrew down the stairs.

'Wonderful, Karl,' I said and I never meant anything more.

Disdainfully he looked at me. I remembered how, after I had retired from wrestling, I said the same thing to him at the top of the stairs at Lane's Club. It was after his bloody battle with Bulldog Bill Garnon—the adjective being used literally.

I saw the same proud disdainful look on his face then as I saw now. But at Lane's Club he hit me full in the face. I fell down a whole flight of steps.

Karl Reginsky of Germany, winner of one of Miss Look's open Tournaments, was only five feet nine inches and fifteen stones but was reckoned with Hungarian Champion, Mike Brendel, as the toughest fighter in the world at the time.

But this time Reginsky glanced at me:

'That's okay, Atholl. I owed it you.' Still disdainful and unsmiling, he slowly turned and walked back to his dressing room.

After the incident at Lane's Club, Reginsky became my firmest friend and even admirer. Why! After I had been taken to hospital detectives asked me for the name of the man who 'assaulted' me. (The word 'assault' always amused me!) Anyone in those days, shoulder or no shoulder, who could knock me down a flight of steps was in my view a real man, so I refused the request. As always, when you refuse to give away a man who is in trouble, you make a friend for life who will go through hell for you. That night Reginsky, at very great personal risk, faced a very ugly crowd over a thousand strong.

The next day the superintendent of police instructed me to call him. He minced no words when he made it quite clear that under no circumstances must I ever again attract such a crowd. 'It was overadvertised,' he said, 'and your wording on the advertisements was exaggerated.'

'Is it possible to exaggerate the Angel!' I asked.

'I'm not arguing with you, Mr. Oakeley,' he replied, 'we cannot have this sort of thing. A crowd of that size may well get out of control. I must ask you, sir, never to do it again.'

Of course he was quite right and I apologised. It is ridiculous to incite such huge crowds to block the streets and unfair to the police who have to control them.

Soon after this the war broke out. This was our last tournament in Manchester.

In 1939 Angel appeared only once more in England. Twenty of Britain's leading surgeons came to see him.

One day after the war ended I invited him to wrestle for me in London. He was always a non-flying Angel so I went to Southampton and met him as he came down the gangway of the Malrretania : a very different Angel to that night in Paris so long ago. Travelling first class and by himself Angel was now heavyweight champion of the world. Crushing opponents five nights a week, with average attendances each night of over 9000, our Angel had made more money in three years than Joe Louis had made in a lifetime.

He was now a millionaire, and so was Karl. They lived in Chicago.

When war had been declared I, as a former regular officer, was on the reserve.

'You go mit us to States,' said Karl. 'We all make million dollars. What for you stay fight in another war just for politicians? You fight in British Army long ago. Mr. Pojello fight in Russian Army.'

'No, Karl,' I replied. 'I stay. You take my percentage. You trained Maurice. He is now your Angel—your Guardian Angel. I stay.'

'You always make big mistakes, Atol. You never listen to Mr. Pojello. You too smart I tink for your boots.'

Much too smart. He was, as usual right.

My services, either in a non-existent front line or even as a qualified army physical training instructor were not required. I was not alone. Six thousand former officers waited six months. Finally we were all summoned to London.

There a little pipsqueak, hardly dry behind the ears, said:

'I'm sorry, Oakeley, we cannot use you. The fighting we anticipated has not materialised. In any case you are out of date. You cannot even form threes, old boy. We should have to train you all over again. And anyway, we've called Hitler's bluff.' Hitler's bluff was called all right—five years later!

I was thinking about all this when I met the Angel in 1947. He put both his arms about me, kissing me on each cheek. Then he turned to the press:

'This man and one other help me when no one else help me. No one then want to know. Now everyone want to know.'

Taught by Karl now he even spoke like him.

A week later Angel appeared at Earls Court. At about that time one of London's leading surgeons approached me. He explained how acromegalians were invariably unable to walk, and Angel was unique in that he still could. . . . It was explained to me that he would get bigger and bigger until his heart gave way under the strain.

Even now the Angel's bone formation had attained terrific proportions. His bones were larger than ever before. But his strength was no longer that of the pre-war Angel.

The surgeons offered him £1000 if he would leave his body for research. But Angel told them he had already left it to the Americans for $10,000.

I went with him to Southampton. He stopped at the gang plank. 'I never forget what you did for me.' Tears were rolling down his great face.

'I did nothing, Maurice. Without Karl none of it would have been possible.'

One afternoon three months later, Pojello felt ill. He went to his room in Chicago, lay down on his bed, and died.

Two hours later Angel came in, Karl was lying face down. Maurice turned him over, and saw that he was dead.

They found the two of them later that night. Poor dear Angel was lying, dead, stretched across the body of the only friend who had ever helped him.

The man, whom the Manchester press had described as 'all the seven dwarfs rolled into one', never deserted his master and benefactor, even in death.

It was inexpressibly sad. The King was dead. And there was no King to follow him!

17. The Post-War Scene: Competition Becomes Exhibition

With Sherry out of the game and Karl and the Angel dead, the postwar wrestling scene was indeed bleak. Kathleen Look was no longer with us. Nearly all the great competitive heavyweights of the pre-war era seemed to have vanished.

The names of Bulldog Bill Garnon, Norman the Butcher, Carver Doone, Karl Reginsky, Karloff Manoogian, Len Franklin and other great pre-war stars no longer appeared on the posters. Only Jack Pye, Bert Assirati and Dave Armstrong seemed to be left, and in the 1950's none of these could be said to be in the first flush of youth.

While all wrestling promotions with which we had been connected had naturally been closed down when war broke out, others had taken the opportunity to promote in our absence. I took the view that if strong men could wrestle in public for money, they could also fight for their country.

After the war we found that some wrestling promotions were being held under 'Mountevans Rules', and that the 'Mountevans' of these rules was none other than Admiral Lord Mountevans himself! We at once obtained a copy of these rules, and found they were an abbreviated copy of our 'All-In' rules of 1930 (which incidentally were my copyright in this country).

Named with Lord Mountevans was a well-known Member of Parliament. We knew that Lord Mountevans, as 'Evans of the Broke', had achieved world-wide admiration. Yet here was this man, a peer of the realm, apparently filching our rules.

The facts were indisputable. One had only to compare the so called 'Mountevans Rules' with ours to see that they were almost identical.

Yet I was informed that neither Mountevans nor the MP concerned had ever been a professional, nor even an amateur, wrestler! Why then had these two become involved?

After travelling north to find out what was going on, I was told that wrestling was now being run as a closed shop, with rights of admission strictly reserved, so eliminating outside challenges. Wrestlers were prohibited from 'working' for any promoter who was not a member of this organisation.

I bought a ticket for one of these so-called 'tournaments' and saw at once that none of the four 'matches' was genuine. Although billed as 'Contests' they were obviously exhibitions. An amateur could have seen through all of them. 'Competitors' escaped from 'Boston Crabs'. One threw his opponent to the ground and then stood back while he got to his feet! Another jerked his opponent's wrist. His adversary at once turned a somersault!!

'What's that throw supposed to be!' I asked the MC.

'Oh, that was the "Irish Whip",' he replied.

I said: 'You must be joking.'

At that moment one of the actors picked up the other in a crotch. He 'body-slammed' him. Then he stood back while the parmer rose to his feet. No attempt was made to follow him down or pin him! Afterwards I spoke to the promoter.

He said: 'We pay for our halls and are legally entitled to reserve the right of admission. So if any of your challengers try to force their way in, or cause a disturbance, they will find themselves in court.'

I replied 'In other words wrestling is no longer to be an open-to all-comers competitive sport but a closed shop!'

'If you want to put it that way, yes. In the past you brought in foreign champions. As a result British boys who wanted to earn a few bob by taking up wrestling could not compete. We think that, as this is a free country, our boys have the right to work in professional wrestling if they want to. We have lots of men. Perhaps by your standards they are not wrestlers but they can put on a good show with plenty of action and that is what the public wants.'

'By publicising bouts as if they were contests are you not representing your bouts as competitive when in reality they are mainly exhibitions!'

'Again, if you want to think that you must do so.'

'Do you realise that all the amateurs will know if bouts are exhibitions?'

'You don't have to tell me anything about amateurs, Atholl Oakeley.'

'Very well then, what happens if someone buys a ticket and then accuses you of fraud? What if it is held that your bouts are billed as contests but in reality are exhibitions?'

'I never said our bouts are exhibitions. If anyone said that, they would have to prove it. Anyway what's wrong with exhibitions! I take the view that, so long as we give the public plenty of action, they won't grumble.'

'In my view anyone and everyone concerned with exhibitions which were billed as contests might well be accessories after the fact. What would you do if the BBC took up wrestling instead of boxing. Then alleged it was a "fake"?'

'Exhibitions are not a "fake". "Fake" is when you bet on the result of a fight when you know that one fighter has been paid to lose or has been threatened with violence, if he doesn't take a dive. We don't arrange our results. We pay our boys good wages. What they do is up to them. We don't want to know. All we ask is a good all action show.

'If results are arranged the press will find out. You know how the papers hate wrestling.

'What can they do? Some wrestler with a grouse may tell them a tale. If this happens and an article appears, a week or two later and everyone will have forgotten it. No one believes what they read in the papers. You ought to know that.'

'And the position of television if they take it up!'

'We can cross that bridge later. If we ever get on TV it won't be your kind of wrestling. It's much too slow. All that sort of amateur stuff is old hat. In wrestling and boxing modern people want action. Boxers and wrestlers who can provide that will get the jobs. You and your giants will be out on your ears.

This conversation was written from notes which I made at the time.

I sent a copy of these to Sherry in America and he wrote back: 'It's the same over here. Guess we're out of date!'

Ignoring these prophecies my next move was to find an arena to replace Bell Vue, as the management seemed no longer interested in proposals from me now that Kathleen had gone.

I approached London's Harringay Arena. After a preliminary canter, I was invited to Promote competitive championship Tournaments.

Jack Solomon was then the promoter for boxing. I became the promoter for wrestling.

The best British professional wrestlers mainly came from Scotland, Cumberland, Westmorland, Durham, Lancashire and Yorkshire. London provided the majority of ex-amateurs.

So again I went North. This time to see my old and valued friend Barnsley's Bert Maasfield.

Every competitive wrestler in the North was known to our Bert-himself a championship-class heavyweight. He informed me that, if I could match the top of the bills at the Arena, he would give me a long list of clever and experienced wrestlers who would fill the preliminary cards. He was enthusiastic about his star pupil, a pitface coal miner (and a relative of his) ring named Frank Mantovitch.

I met Frank and saw at once that here was the post-war British heavyweight whom I had been looking for. I had already heard rumours in the softer South of a great Yorkshire heavyweight, but had taken this to refer to Mansfield.

'Manto' was as tough as they come. Most weightlifters only think they are strong, and so they are for thirty seconds at a time. But the work this man had to do, which consisted of heaving out coal from the pitface for hour after hour, would have given all the weightlifters whom I knew a coronary. In addition Frank was an international class championship heavyweight. Thus a new star was born. But without Bert's knowledge of all the wrestlers Harringay Tournaments could not have survived even with Jack Doyle's drawing power.

So, having matched the preliminaries, I wrote to Mr. Molotov mentioning I was a friend of the great Russian wrestler, Karl Pojello. I asked him if he would allow the Soviet heavyweight champion and champion of Bulgaria, Ivan Georgieff; to wrestle for me in London.

Mr. Molotov courteously agreed but made the condition that the GRA and I, whenever Georgieff came over, would ensure that he returned to East Berlin where he was practising as a surgeon. Having given our word on this, I made a point personally of seeing Georgieff off on his plane whenever he left England.

In spite of troubles and tribulations, the Harringay Tournament was a great success. We put up the House Full boards, and 10,500 people paid for admission. Mr. Gentle and his directors were impressed. They had expected an attendance of around two thousand.

I waited some time before promoting my next tournament. There seemed still to be an acute shortage everywhere in Europe and USA of championship-class heavyweights. But in spite of all the difficulties I managed eventually to obtain entries from stars like Alex Cadier (former Olympic double titleholder and champion of Sweden), Primo Carnera, world champion Frank Sexton of USA, Larry Gains, Martinschenok and Georgieff of Russia, together with other foreign and British stars, so I eventually got the tournaments under way.

Of the British athletes, Frank Mantovitch became, as anticipated, the new British champion. He and Bert Mansfield took on all challengers, and they were a good pair.

But although we drew five or six thousand for each tournament, so far, with the exception of the first Harringay Tournament, the huge crowds who used to pay to see Jack Sherry, Karl Pojello, Sergei Kalmikoff, Karl Reginsky, Carver Doone, Norman the Butcher, Mike Brendel, Kola Kwariani, Karloff Manoogian and myself had never really materialised.

It may well be that Group Captain Wilson secretly had a soft spot for me in my efforts to build up wrestling in their Arena, despite the growing opposition of the exhibition wrestling game. For one day he called me to his office.

'For a place of this size,' he said: 'You need a known drawing card. There are 90,000 Irishmen in London. I suggest you go and see Jack Doyle. I understand he can wrestle as well as box.' I did as I was told and went to see Jack Doyle.

I had heard in America from Jack Dempsey that Doyle was the hardest hitter in boxing, but that he appeared unwilling to stand up to really hard training and some thought he was unreliable. But Wladek and Stanislaus told me that he had had wrestling training, as had most American heavyweight boxers.

I knew all about Doyle. He had been in the Irish Guards and had been discovered by Len Harvey, one of our finest boxers and a great champion.

The story at that time was that the Boxing Board of Control had fined Doyle £500. It was said that the Irishman was only paid £2000 for his box-fight with Eddie Phillips. As I heard it, £48,000 was taken at the box office and Doyle had insisted on being paid £2000 in advance. When the fight ended (more abruptly than some people expected) Jack, plus his £2000, flew to Mexico.

Jack Doyle was certainly a wonderful-looking man. Six foot five and nineteen stone, he stood as straight as a ramrod, as do all the Guards. I felt three foot nothing in front of this magnificent person with the dignity and bearing of Richard Coeur de Lion.

'Good morning,' I said. 'Can you wrestle?'

'Sure I can and what is that to you?'

'Will you wrestle at Harringay Arena?'

'And who for, may I ask?'
'For me.'
'I will if you're after paying properly.'
'I pay percentage...' and Jack signed his contract.

Again on the advice of my friend Group Captain Wilson, my next move was to go down to see Eddie Phillips at Bow. He was very strongly built for a boxer. I found him to be a very straightforward man. The local police thought the world of him. He had the reputation of never having taken part in a fixed boxing match.

I made it clear that this match was on the level. Eddie said, 'Naturally, but please realise I know very little about wrestling. I will ask the police here to train me and do my best.'

When the news was released that the 'darlin' boy' of the entire British national press was to wrestle for Atholl Oakeley, the storm broke. Everyone wanted to know where Doyle would set up his training camp.

We arranged for a friend to tip newsmen off that he would train in Scotland. But one man, who knew me, decided that this was a bluff. In fact we all believed that this man, the one and only Peter Wilson (about my only friend on the nationals), knew where we were going and that it was not to Scotland.

Accompanied by my strong six-foot son, John Oakeley, I took Jack and a sparring partner by train to Minehead. From there we went by car miles out to a lonely farmhouse on Exmoor, far away from telephone, pub or post office. 'Nothing but sheep,' as Jack said on arrival.

I must admit that I have seldom seen anyone so angry as Jack Doyle was when he saw where we had brought him. There was no electric light and I will never forget the sight of this great man in his hundred-guinea suit walking up the stairs holding a candle and cursing like mad.

Finding that he was constantly watched (so as to ensure that he could not try to 'escape'), Doyle resigned himself to his fate. We posted a sentry on the hill outside the farmhouse to sound the alarm if Peter Wilson found us. But no one came.

Day after day we practised Half Nelsons, wrist locks and all the rest. Every day Jack looked better and became fitter and stronger.

Only once did he try to give us the slip. He had slightly hurt his knee so I allowed him to rest while John, the sparring partner and I went out running. On our way back we were overtaken by an estate car going up the lane to our lonely farmhouse. Twenty minutes later, still apparently empty except for the driver, the car returned, going slowly down the very narrow lane. John suddenly ran after it and jumped up to look through the rear window. There was Doyle, crouched on the floor.

At dinner Jack was giving us an account of all his American exploits. John said, 'Did you have a car!'

'Sure and of course I did. A foine great Cadillac so it was.'

'Where did you sit, Jack?'

'I had a chauffeur. I sat in the back.'

'Under the seat like this afternoon!' asks John, and shoots out of the room like a rabbit with the Gorgeous Gael in full cry after him.

We returned Jack in marvellous shape to London. He looked every inch a champion. A capacity crowd of 10,600 people thronged into the Arena for the match.

Eddie, trained by the police at Bow, was heavily backed. He fought a game and plucky fight, but he knew very little of wrestling. Doyle fought better than I had expected, but he found Phillips was strong and tough. The match in consequence was rather slow. Doyle eventually won on a disqualification. At once one or two boxing writers hinted it had been faked. I found this idiotic. Both men were boxers and we all know that British boxers never arrange fights. Why then should these two arrange one now?

Phillips, known to the G.R.A. directors and the police as a 100 per cent honest man, would not have lost for Doyle no matter what he had been offered. Had he deliberately done so he would have lost his backers at Bow thousands of pounds. The Irish came en masse to see their idol, and Doyle would have died rather than lose to Phillips. The match, like all Doyle's subsequent fights, was rather slow, but always perfectly genuine. The public realised this and came to see him in ever increasing numbers, just as Group Captain Wilson had said they would.

Having matched two boxers I rather wanted to see how an Irish fighter would fare against a great American champion who had nearly won the world boxing championship. So I brought over 'Two Ton' Tony Gallento from NewJersey, USA.

There was another huge crowd. Gallento won, breaking two of Jack's ribs and sending him to St. Mary's Hospital. Gallento had a supreme contempt for Doyle so later I rematched them in Dublin. Jack wished to fight Gallento again, this time in front of his own people. The fight drew a huge gate of 22,500 people! Jack was holding Gallento by the foot. Both were down on the mat. Suddenly Tony used his other foot to give Doyle an almighty shove. Whether he intended Jack to fall on the concrete I do not know. I hope not and believe not. But as Jack went hurtling out he held onto Gallento's foot. The Irishman went clear and fell on a chair but Tony's head hit the concrete and he lay still, out to the world!

At once all the Irish round the ringside were pushing the half-stunned Doyle with everything within reach. He climbed back into the ring just as Tony Melrose reached a count of seventeen. (Twenty seconds are allowed for matmen to return to the ring after ejection.)

Jack stood up, dazed, and was given the decision. But Gallento woke up some ten minutes later in the dressing room. I heard that when he returned to New Jersey all the small boys shouted, 'look out, Tony, Jack Doyle's waiting for you.'

That night I found Jack paying for drinks to all Dublin, it seemed. He had a large sum due to him. As I came into the hotel he came up, put his arm round my shoulders, and in an imperious voice said: 'And would your Grace be after letting me have some money?'!!

I had no intention of allowing him to waste his hard-earned money buying drinks for all and sundry. I asked:

'How much do you want to go on with?'

'Sure and 'tis fifty poonds would do for now.'

I handed him a five-pound note. Never will I forget the way he drew himself up to his full height. Looking like my former headmaster addressing a boy who had rifled the poor box, Doyle said in a commanding voice and for all to hear:

'How dare you, sir. Would ye be after offerin' me, Jack Doyle, such a pittance? I asked you, sir, for money, not cigar money. I shall ignore you. You oughter wear your collar back to front. You're not a promoter at all at all. Sure and 'tis the Archbishop of Hamble ye are.' He then handed the note to the barman and said: 'Give the Archbishop a cigar.'

Ever after that he addressed all his letters to me: 'The Archbishop of Hamble'.

18. The Long, the Short, and The Tallest of Them All

In fairness to the national press I must by and large admit that, led by my old friend Peter Wilson, they really gave some excellent publicity for the 'Gorgeous Gael'. One journalist acidly remarked:

'At least where Doyle is concerned we can write what we like without being sued.'

Jack had a tremendous sense of humour. One day a Sunday paper sent a woman to interview Jack. If genuine wrestlers detested male boxing writers as a class their dislike of them was as nothing to their contempt for young women journalists who came around and asked silly questions in 'Haw Haw' voices. As is the custom in most modern interviews, the questions were both leading and loaded. Firstly a statement of fact' (which was not a fact at all) was made by the interviewer. Then, in context with this statement, a leading question was asked.

In this way the journalist first assumed, incorrectly, that wrestling was faked. This in itself was absurd, as no woman journalist would have the slightest idea whether any fight was fixed or otherwise. Even expert boxers and wrestlers cannot always be certain, except possibly when a man is counted out when unmarked and sitting down, or when dropping from a blow which would not knock out a baby. Then they may draw their own conclusions. But one can assume that, before derogatory opinions are publicly voiced by former professional world champions, they first consider all the implications.

The question that the woman asked Doyle was:

'How do you make all the blood!' Which quite incorrectly assumed that the blood was made.

Jack in his most puckish mood replied:

'Sure 'tis a capsule filled with cochineal I put in my ear. Then when I get in a head lock the capsule breaks so cochineal goes all over my head so it does!'

The editor, who may not have read it, passed this. So he received a letter from me asking for an immediate and unqualified withdrawal together with an apology. I explained in my letter why the suggestion was ridiculous and intended as a silly answer to a silly young woman.

To his credit the editor printed a full retraction, and wrote personally to me expressing his regrets for the publication. In my reply I thanked him and gave the following reasons for my complaint:

1. Doyle was under exclusive contract to me. As an ex-amateur and former captain of the British amateur international wrestling team I allowed no faking or pre-arrangement of any kind.

2. It was absolutely impossible for a gelatine capsule tough and strong enough to hold cochineal to be broken by a head lock. Any headlock pressure would only ram it down the ear without breaking it.

One day I was talking to the great Irish promoter, Gerald Egan, who told me of another great Irish heavyweight. This was the Irish giant Jim Culley, who stood seven foot seven inches in his stockinged feet. Culley was so tall that he had to stoop when he walked down the tunnels to the Tube stations to avoid banging his head on the lights.

I matched him against that great American Eddie Virag. To everyone's surprise, including my own, Virag, weighing only sixteen stone and standing a mere six foot, defeated the giant!

The London public had never before seen a heavyweight fighter of the height and size of Culley.

They had thought Carver Doone the ultimate. Then Ivan Georgieff, even more enormous, eclipsed Carver. Now Jim Culley, a whole head taller than Georgieff, made them wonder where this giant business was going to end. But Jim Culley was only the penultimate in giant wrestlers.

Another, greater than ever before, was soon to fight in England. In fact this giant would be the greatest Colossus to appear in London since Angus McAskell, from the Isle of Man, appeared before Queen Elizabeth in the sixteenth century. A new giant who would make all other wrestlers and boxers look like children. A fantastic monster of a man of enormous stature and fabulous weight. During Jack's debut in wrestling, I heard someone remark:

'Oh, Jack Doyle is Atholl Oakeley's drawing card. He may not arrange results but he takes damned good care to match him against easy opponents.'

Only by good luck had Jack gained a decision over the great Tony Gallento because, as the doctors testified, Gallento was knocked out cold when his head hit the concrete floor. Being concussed he had been unable to continue the fight.

I felt that the time had come to find out what Jack Doyle could do against one of my greatest giants.

I knew that if a fighter used his brains, he should be able to beat a giant. Anyone, who, like Doyle, could spring from little or nothing and earn a hundred thousand pounds, could be no fool. So off I went to find the greatest of all giants. This time really the greatest of all living giants, Kurt Zehe.

6 ft 7 in Camera had told me that Zehe was a massive Hercules who had recently won the German heavyweight championship. This new Colossus, he said, lived in Frankfurt. Zehe was not quite so tall as Rhinehardt, the 9 ft 6 in giant who lived in Rotterdam. But he was far heavier and much stronger.

Once before I had tried to contract Rhinehardt. Jim Noice (who was a champion middleweight in 'All In' and 'Judo') went over at my request to see this Dutch giant and ascertain if he would wrestle.

Jim duly arrived in Rotterdam. There in the street he met the giant riding on his gigantic bicycle. At the traffic lights, Rhinehardt dismounted. Jim, unable to speak the language, boldly clasped him round one leg and held on. A crowd collected but the day was saved when Mr. Rhinehardt senior, who spoke English, arrived. Jimmie took them both out to dinner. The giant ate thirty plates of soup and then, after all that, he decided he would not wrestle.

With 'Two Tan' Tony Gallento and his American manager I went over to Brussels, where we arranged with Mr. Robyns, the Belgian promoter, to meet this super giant.

Zehe's entrance was dramatic. We were all sitting in the hotel lounge, drinking coffee, when suddenly the door opened and in he came. He had to bend down and turn sideways to go through the doorway! When he stood up I saw at once this was indeed the greatest of the giants. Here was no Carver Doone, Georgieff or Culley, but a real Behemoth.

We took him to the gymnasium and weighed and measured him.

Height	8 ft 4 in
Weight	751 English pounds (fifty stone)
Chest	110 inches
Legs	31/2 feet around
Biceps	30 inches
Boots	Equivalent to size 30
Width of shoulders	3 feet seam to seam.

I tried on the jacket of this Brobdingnagian. It reached down to the ground!

We got Picture Post to take a picture of an eight-year-old boy sitting in one of Zehe's boots. These, incidentally, were hand-made and cost over a hundred pounds. (£500 at today's values.)

Eighteen stone Tony Gallento would not have his photo taken with this vast wrestler at first, but finally he relented.

I thought: 'This is the man for Doyle. I wonder what Jack will say when he sees him!'

So a contract was drawn up and arrangements made for this super-giant to fight in London.

The only hotel which would take my gigantic friend was Russell Square's Imperial. There we put three double beds into Room 250, where I had formerly booked Georgieff: but we had to get permission to book a double room for a single person as this was then against police rules.

The press turned up in force, and there were a hundred photographers at the Imperial.

'Have you a hobby?' asked one newsman.

'I mak conjuring,' says the giant in a bass voice.

'Show us some,' say the journalists.

Kurt blew out the electric lamp over his head.

Everyone thought a conjuring giant was an excellent thing!

I asked Kurt later how he did it. He showed me a switch behind and above the door. No one else was tall enough to see it!

Doyle was not too happy when he first saw Kurt, but with his usual Irish courage, he agreed to go through with the match. He trained hard and at last his great night and greater opponent arrived.

The giant put one tremendous foot on the top step leading up to the ring. It broke at once followed by all the other steps underneath.

However, with his usual forethought, Group Captain Wilson had had the ring reinforced. It had to stand up to seventy stone!

Taking off his dressing gown the Colossus, billed by me as 'Gargantua', stood quite still as he literally towered over Doyle. He looked like Ben Nevis. Doyle engaged him, and at once, as gently as if he was picking up a little boy, Kurt lifted Jack off his feet and gently laid him down. He then lay on him. Time four minutes.

Jack shouted blue murder. The referee, looking like a pygmy between two dinosaurs, asked Gargantua to stand up. Not tall enough to lift up his hand the referee pointed to him then raised his own! Afterwards I asked Jack why he made such a hullabaloo.

'Glory be, Archbishop,' he replied. ''Tis yourself would have made a bloody noise with a damned great Centurian tank on top of you.'

After this I took Kurt to Eire. The railway authorities argued that he took up too much room and attracted too much attention. They said I must take him First Class or they would not carry him. So I made them look up the original Railways Act. This laid down that they had to carry a fare-paying passenger.

When I pointed this out, someone said, 'When that was written around 1830 no one expected Atholl Oakeley to arrive with a fifty-stone, eight-foot-high giant who took up half a carriage !'

On the ship he was unable to pass through the door of any of the cabins, so we covered him with a rug and he lay like a fallen fir tree on the saloon settee. He was rather shy and pulled the dark covering over his head. I thought he looked like a landlocked whale.

The Daily Telegraph devoted a whole column of its front page to him, and even the BBC made a short film in spite of his being a wrestler.

One day I took Kurt to the London Pavilion. Followed by a crowd of about a thousand we went to the box office. But the cashier refused to sell us tickets on the grounds that the giant was too big for the seats. Luckily we met Peter Wilson, who said, 'Atholl, where on earth do you dig these fellows up?' Peter got us in. I sat one side of the aisle, Kurt sat in the aisle, taller than people standing up, and Peter sat in a seat the other side. These giants are good natured but they do make life difficult.

One interview was quite amusing.

'Were you in the war!' asked a Dublin journalist.

'Jah,' says Kurt.

'How did you fare!' asks the pressman.

'I captured was.'

'Great Scott, who on earth ever captured you!'

'I sleep. Mit mein Kalnarads I in a dug-out sleep. "Achtung Kurt", they say. Then I see many Canadian soldiers into our dug-out come. "Hands up, Fritz", they say and point guns. All stand mit hands up. Then I stand up and Canadian soldiers put down guns and put their hands up.'

'So you were taken prisoner?'

'Yah.'
'Were you glad or sorry?'
'Glad. Too big target.'
But now my time was drawing to a close. Harringay Arena was a very expensive place to run. Soon the writing was on the wall.
One morning I went into Group Captain Wilson's office. Billy Graham had packed the Arena the previous night.
'Have you been saved, Oakeley?' asked the Group Captain. 'No, sir,' I replied, 'I was not able to attend last night.'
'Well we have. Billy Graham has taken the Arena for three months.'
Shortly afterwards, the wonderful Harringay Arena was sold and converted into a grocery storehouse. So I transferred the tournaments to the Royal Albert Hall. Having managed, when everyone else had failed, to obtain LCC permission to Promote wrestling here, I found that over a thousand 'seat holders' could watch without paying. At the best the paying customers could not exceed some 5000.

Wrestling was rapidly deteriorating into acrobatic exhibitions. After a spectacular fight between a smaller giant, the American ranch-owner, Ski hi Lee, six foot ten inches, and the brilliant South African champion, Tiger Joe Robinson (one of the finest fights ever seen in London), I promoted one or two other tournaments, finally having a flaming row with a contestant whom we disqualified for not trying.

I refused to pay this man and he put the matter in the hands of his solicitors. I went to see them. On explaining how I was able to tell if a wrestler or boxer was not trying they agreed that my word on this would be acceptable to most courts, and I heard no more.

Now that the arena was smaller, and heavyweights of championship calibre few and far between, I decided to stop flogging the dying horse of competition wrestling. 'Right of admission strictly reserved' had never appeared on my posters and never would!

If the public preferred commercial exhibitions, interposed with some genuine matches, that was their affair. If they really believed that you could take a man's hand or wrist and, with a quick jerk, me.

My baby has now grown into a forty-year-old giant. As I forecast it has forced professional boxing into the background.

Four million people each week watch this sport, and both men and women enjoy its thrills. No other individual sport attracts such a terrific audience. It needs no state aid to stand upon its own feet. It needs and gets no medals. As entertainment it stands alone.

When I first took Tony Sherlock, a friend from Eton, into Islington's Ashdown Club fifty years ago, wrestling audiences numbered twelve if we were lucky. It took many of us many years to bring wrestling back again as England's major and oldest individual sport.

But it pains me still that pure exhibition wrestling has now taken over completely and so I close this book of giants with Cory's poem:

'They told me, Heraclitus, they told me you were dead.
They brought me bitter news to hear and bitter tears to shed.
I wept as I remembered how often you and I
had tired the sun with talking
and sent him down the sky.'